DATING,
DINING,
DANCING,
AND OTHER
TEEN
DILEMMAS

Dear Alfie & Mel,

I hope you enjoy reading this book as much as I did writing it. May the Lord bless you in all your righteous endeavor.

Much love,
Miriam
Clarl

DATING, DINING, DANCING, AND OTHER TEEN DILEMMAS

VIVIAN R. CLINE

ILLUSTRATIONS BY
THOMAS R. LEISHMAN

BOOKCRAFT
Salt Lake City, Utah

Library of Congress Catalog Card Number: 94-71366
ISBN 0-88494-931-1

First Printing, 1994

Printed in the United States of America

This book is dedicated to all those youth (and those who think young) who read it with the desire for self-improvement. May you discover that real class is an action of love and respect toward others and not a measure of money or social status.

CONTENTS

ACKNOWLEDGMENTS

I would like to give special thanks to my loving and eternal companion, S. Douglas Cline. I would have never accomplished the things I have without his support and encouragement. And to my five beautiful children, Talmadge, Walter, Burgess, Audrey, and Autumn. Through years of traveling and speaking they have never complained but have shared in the happiness I feel in teaching and helping others. To my wonderful parents, Gold Tate and Margaret Reynolds, who taught me traditional Southern courtesies and manners. To Belva Cline, my dear, sweet mother-in-law, who first suggested I write a book and who never gave up on me. To Joyce Smith, my seminary teacher, who taught me as a teenager in her lovely home the importance of proper dining. To Carol Warnick, my dear college roommate who took me by the hand and walked me through the doors of Bookcraft, then patiently pre-edited my manuscript so it was legible. And last of all I acknowledge with gratitude my Father in Heaven for allowing me the opportunity to learn by study and by error and then to share that knowledge with my brothers and sisters here on earth.

CHAPTER ONE

INTRODUCTIONS
AND
FIRST IMPRESSIONS

Have you ever done something stupid? I mean, really dumb and embarrassing? For example, there, standing at the end of the hall, is that special girl or guy you have been dying to meet. You see her leaning against a locker to visit with a friend, and you begin to feel your temperature rise. If you stay in your current walking pattern

1

down the hall, you will surely pass in front of her. What if she looks at you? What if she smiles? What if she *speaks?* This could be it—your one and only chance to meet and impress her.

Your confidence rises, and you quickly decide that this is the day. It's now or never! Your path is steady and your walk calm and controlled as you cruise down the hall. Thoughts are racing through your mind with clever things you could say.

Suddenly, you are there. You slow your walk down and look at her in hopes that your eyes will meet.

Oh no! She turns away from her friend, and there you are, face-to-face. Your palms are wet, the pit that was in your stomach now drops to your feet, and you freeze. Your mouth is open, but no words will come out. Your prospective friend looks at you, smiles, and walks away. Did you just blow it royally or what?

One of the most important steps in establishing a relationship with someone is to make a dynamite first impression. Remember, you never get a second chance to make a first impression. The opinions others initially form of you have a tendency to be lasting ones. If you have made a favorable first impression on someone and he later hears something negative about you, he probably won't believe it. It works the other way as well. If someone forms a negative impression of you and then hears something positive about you, he probably won't believe that, either.

There are four things to remember when you meet someone for the first time. First, straighten your back and hold your head erect. This is a nonverbal way of saying, "I'm confident." Are you? Probably not. You may even be scared to death, but the other person doesn't have to know that. A rule of thumb that I use quite often is "Fake it till you make it." You see, as a person thinks of himself, so is he. You begin by telling yourself you are confident, then acting and looking like you are confident, and, eventually, you become confident. Thus, "Fake it till you make it."

The second thing to remember is to look people you are meeting straight in the eyes. This shows them that they are important to you and that they have your undivided attention. When you look away from people you are meeting for the first time, they sometimes feel they aren't very important, because if they were, you wouldn't be so easily distracted. Even if you are terribly shy, try to look people directly in the eyes.

Third, have a pleasant expression on your face. This is a sign that you are a positive and happy person. Are you happy? Maybe not today. Maybe you just wrecked your dad's new car—or maybe the date you wanted to take to prom just got asked by someone else. You aren't in the greatest of moods. But do you still smile? Yes. You see, the person you are meeting doesn't know you yet and couldn't care less about your personal problems. They just care about how you make them feel. So smile.

Last of all, extend a warm greeting. If the person is your own age, simply say, "Hi, Joe Cool. It's nice to meet you." Another option would be, "Hey, Joe. How are you doing?" Do whatever is the cool and accepted greeting in your area. If you are meeting an adult, however, you will want to extend a more respectful and dignified greeting, such as: "How do you do, Mrs. Brown. It's a pleasure to meet you." "How do you do" can be formal or informal, is casual, and is always acceptable. To an adult, it says you have class. Immediately her opinion of you will go up by at least ten points!

Please remember to always address an adult by her last name until she requests that you call her by her first name. This not only shows respect but allows the adult the prerogative of deciding what she wants you to call her. If she says, "Oh, please, call me Susan," then you should respond by saying, "Yes. Thank you, Susan."

Never address someone your own age with "How do you do." They will immediately think you're a weirdo and will have absolutely nothing to do with you!

Introducing people can be uncomfortable if you are

3

not quite sure of the rules. There are three basic rules that you need to remember.

Rule number one is to say the name of the lady first. If you have a friend who is a girl and you are introducing her to your friend who is a guy, you would say, for example, "Tiffany, I want you to meet a bud of mine. This is Matt."

The second rule is to say the name of the older person first. If you were introducing your mother to Tiffany, you would say, "Mother, I would like you to meet a friend of mine. This is Tiffany."

Third and most important of the three rules is to say the name of the most important person first. This overrides the previous two rules. For example, if you were going to introduce your mother to the governor of your state, you would say, "Governor Jones, I would like you to meet my mother, Mrs. Brown." This shows respect for his high position.

When introducing two people for the first time, it is the responsibility of the person doing the introducing to say something about one, if not both, of the people being introduced. Most people just say, "Tiffany, this is Matt. Matt, this is Tiffany." Not only is this a cold introduction, but it leaves both people to wonder, *Who cares?* A much better introduction would be, "Tiffany, I would like you to meet a close friend of mine who I play basketball with. This is Matt. Matt, I want you to meet one of the best-looking girls in my math class. Not only is she beautiful, she's brainy, too."

This introduction has just done two things. It has complimented each of the two friends who are now meeting and has given them two topics of conversation, basketball and math class.

When you are meeting someone for the first time, make sure you say his or her name at least three times during your conversation. Not only does it show that you cared enough to remember the name, but once you have said it three times, chances are you won't forget it.

Oh no! What if you don't remember someone's name?

4

A friend whom you haven't seen since elementary school comes up to you in the mall and says, "Hi, Joe. How are you?" Suddenly you freeze and turn all available computer banks in your mind on full blast. The thought *How do I know this person?* sends impulses throughout your brain searching for data.

In my research on etiquette and social skills I have found that many of the etiquette books teach something I disagree with. They say that if you meet someone you don't remember, you should say, "Excuse me—you do look familiar, but I can't seem to recall your name."

Put yourself in the place of that person for just a minute. How would you feel if an old friend whom you once felt close to didn't remember you? Real important, right? You would probably feel embarrassed and want to shrink and say to yourself, *Oh, I'm no one important, just little ole Susan. No one remembers me!*

There is one rule of thumb that I feel overrides every rule of etiquette ever invented: to make others feel comfortable. This is the reason social skills came about in the first place.

Think about it for a minute. The objective in eating our food is to get it from the plate into our stomachs. Why don't we take our hand, fill it full of food, and smash it into our mouths? Our goal would be accomplished, but look what we have done in the process—we have totally grossed out everyone at our table.

We don't learn social skills so we can show others we are classy because we know the right thing to do and they are not because they don't. The only difference may be that we have had the opportunity to learn that skill and they haven't—yet!

I have found that the best thing to do when you can't remember someone, or at least their name, is, again, to "fake it till you make it." Ask questions that might jog your memory, such as, "Wow, I haven't seen you forever. How long has it been?" or "Wow, you're looking great. What are you doing these days?"

Ideally their response to these questions will help you recall how you knew the person and you can carry on a coherent conversation. If you still don't remember, just act happy that he remembered you.

If you think you will probably never see him again, be cordial and just say, "It was great to see you again. Maybe we'll run into each other again sometime. Take care!" But if it is someone you really do want to keep in touch with, you need to be sure to get his name. One clever trick is to say, "Hey, this isn't going to work. We need to get together and catch up on things. Put your name and phone number down on this piece of paper [grab the nearest piece of paper you can find—napkin, gum wrapper, anything] and I'll give you a call."

As soon as he writes down his name and number, quickly look at it. Presto! Now you have his name. Then say in parting, "It was super to see you again, Tom. We'll be in touch."

Starting a conversation is easy when someone has introduced you correctly. You automatically have a topic to pick up on. How do you start a conversation, though, if there is no topic to pick up on and no one knows you?

A classic example of this is when you are at a party with a date or a friend and he takes off for a few minutes, leaving you behind. What are you supposed to do? How about picking someone out, going up to her, extending your hand, and saying, "Hello, my name is Linda. Who are you?" If you try this approach, you'll soon find that everyone will treat you like the plague!

You see, you have just done two no-no's. First, you have assumed the person wants to meet you, and maybe she doesn't. The message you just sent is, "I'm very important, and I'm just sure you want to meet me."

The second mistake is that you have invaded her space. Believe it or not, everyone has his own space. If you want to see this for sure, take your hand and hold it about six inches away from the hand of a friend. Now gradually bring your hand closer to hers. As you get an inch or two away from her hand, you will feel a strange vibration or aura. Almost everyone has this aura, and no one likes someone else to invade it unless he has been invited. Never just come up and introduce yourself to someone. You must break the ice first.

One easy way to do this is to bounce the conversation ball out into the group by making a comment about the food or the decor. For example, you might say, "This punch is incredible. Does anyone know what's in it?" If someone wants to strike up a conversation, she will jump in with a comment like, "I don't know, but I would sure like to find out."

Another way to start a conversation is to pay someone a compliment. Make sure it's sincere. People hate phonies. You might comment about a ring by saying, "That's a really cool ring you are wearing. Did you find it around here?"

Once the ice has been broken with a short conversation, then you can say, "By the way, my name is Linda." The other person will almost always say her name, and then you can respond with "It's nice to meet you."

Whatever comment you make to start the conversation, make sure it's positive. No one likes someone who is negative and always complaining. That's the type of person others often stay away from!

After you meet someone for the first time, it's nice, though not necessary, to go back to that person before leaving and say you were glad to meet her. Make a brief comment about whatever it was that the two of you spoke about. This is going the extra mile, but the message it sends is that you're a thoughtful and caring person.

Remember that first impressions are lasting ones. Follow the guidelines we've discussed in this chapter, and be yourself. Be positive, and don't forget the overriding rule of thumb for all social skills: Make the other person feel comfortable—even if you have to break a rule!

CHAPTER TWO

TELEPHONE SKILLS

We often have a love/hate relationship with the telephone. We love the phone when we are called by that special person we have been waiting patiently to hear from. On the other hand, don't you just hate it when the phone rings and you're in the shower? You dash out in a panic, trying to make sure you reach the phone before the answering machine clicks in. There you stand in all your glory. You're dripping wet and your towel is about to fall off, bringing total embarrassment for sure! With all the composure you can muster, you pick up the phone and say in your calmest and most impressive voice, "Hello?"

Suddenly you hear a computer voice say, "Hello. My name is Bill. I want to be your milkman." Does that totally chap you or what? You replace the phone in a not-so-gentle manner, and as you drip all the way back to the bathroom you rail on yourself for even getting out of the shower to answer it. But you realize there really was a chance that it was that special person who had called, and you know you would do it all over again.

Because the telephone is such an important part of communication in our lives, we need to be aware of some guidelines that will make it more beneficial and comfortable to use.

Always answer the phone in a pleasant tone of voice. Smile and say, "Hello." If you're wondering why you have to smile before you answer the phone, it's because the expression on your face is reflected in the tone of your voice.

Try this little experiment: Put a frown on your face and say, "Hello." Did you hear the tone of voice you just projected? Probably it was gruff and the inflection of your voice went down on the last syllable.

Now put a smile on your face and say it again. You will notice that this time your voice has more energy and that the inflection went up on the last syllable.

Has this ever happened at your house? You're in the kitchen with your mom, and she's railing on you for something. Maybe your room is a disaster. Maybe you borrowed her car and forgot to put gas in it, and it ran out while she was on the freeway. She's really mad, and she's letting you know!

Suddenly the phone rings. Your mom stops in the middle of her fit, puts a smile on her face, and says the sweetest little "Hello." As soon as the call is over, she hangs up the phone and reverts to her original mad tone of voice.

Question: Is your mother being a fake? The answer is no, she is not. Your mother is simply being courteous to the person on the other end of the line. The caller couldn't care less what kind of personal problems your mom is having. She just wants to remind her of her meeting Wednesday night.

When you answer the phone and the caller asks for you, you respond by identifying yourself. Girls should say, "Yes, this is she." Guys should say, "Yes, this is he." Though saying *her* or *him* may seem right, it is grammatically incorrect.

If you answer and the call is for someone else, the correct response should be, "Yes, just a moment, please." Put the receiver down or press the mute button and get the person they asked for. Never scream out, "Mother, telephone!" This totally destroys the eardrums of the person on the other end.

If the person they asked for is not there, say, "I'm sorry, but she's not here. May I take a message, please?" Make sure you write down the name of the person who called, the date and time of the call, a number where they can be reached, and a message, if there is one.

There are only a few cases in which it is appropriate to hang up on the caller. They are as follows—

Answering machines: I love having an answering machine because I don't miss most phone calls. Just speak to the machine like you would to a person. Leave your name, number, a brief message, and then say good-bye. If you are really uncomfortable with that, however, you may just hang up.

Obscene calls: Never say anything back to them. You will just add fuel to the fire. Simply hang up.

Incoherent two-year-olds: We have a rule in our house that I hope you have in yours. Anyone can answer the phone provided they can say, "Hello. Yes. Just a minute, please." Obviously the call is not going to be for a small child, so the child's responsibility is to get the person the caller wants. Most children can handle that, but if they can't and get carried away in telling you about their Cabbage Patch Kids, hang up.

Telephone recordings: There's got to be a better way to advertise than by annoying people with recordings. Hang up.

Telephone solicitors: After they have identified what they are selling, you may simply cut in and say, "I'm sorry, but we wouldn't be interested. Thank you." Then hang up.

Never ask, "Who is this?" It is too direct and sounds nosy. If you need to find out who's calling, say, "May I ask who's calling, please?" If you ask politely, the caller will almost always tell you.

When you are the one calling, you may say either, "Hello. May I speak with Gina, please?" or "Hello. This is Chad Hoffman calling. May I speak with Gina, please?"

It isn't necessary to identify yourself, but I have found it to be most helpful. By giving your name, you've avoided the obvious question of who is calling. The person you are calling can now pick up the phone and say, "Hello, Chad. How are you doing?" and not have to wonder who's on the other end.

Normally the person who places the call should be the one to end it. Sometimes, however, when a friend wants to talk forever, you might want to politely say that you would love to visit longer but you need to go. You should then arrange another time when you can visit.

A modern convenience is Call Waiting. Please remember that its purpose is to let your caller get in touch with you more easily. It is extremely rude to put a caller on hold in order to catch another call and then not return to him for five minutes. That's a sure message that the second caller was far more important.

When using Call Waiting, simply say, "Excuse me, please, while I catch that other call." Quickly answer the second caller. Say that you are on the other line and that you will be happy to return the call in just a few minutes. Now click back to your first caller and apologize for the interruption. Start the conversation back with a question relating to the subject where you left off.

Remember that a telephone is an important means of communication. It helps you get a message to someone in a very short time. For this reason, try to make your phone calls relatively brief. Accomplish the purpose for your call. Then, if you want to just visit, tell your friend that you would like to go over or have your friend come over. Don't tie up the line for lengthy periods of time. You might miss a call from that special person!

CHAPTER THREE

DATING ETIQUETTE

Dating is a subject that is first and foremost on the minds of many teenagers. How do you ask someone out? How do you treat her or him? How do you end the date? How do you act so that you don't look like a fool?

If these questions sound all too familiar, you are going to love this chapter! We will discuss not only the answers to these questions but also many other things that will help you be more at ease in the dating game.

I am dividing this chapter into three sections: extending the invitation, dating courtesies, and ending the date (that is, how to say good-bye or good night).

Extending the Invitation

Typically in the dating game, women have been at the disadvantage because it's usually the men who do the asking. However, nowadays there are a lot of occasions when it is appropriate for the girls to do the inviting.

Girls' choice dances, Sadie Hawkins dates, and women's week occasions are but a few.

Guys seem to enjoy girls' choice dates because they help relieve the financial burden other special dates bring them. Being the mother of three teenage sons, I can attest to the fact that they would go to almost every dating event possible if it weren't for all the money it costs.

So how do you get a date?

The plain and simple answer to that is, you have to let the other person know you are interested!

There are good things and bad things on television these days. One bad thing TV teaches is that in order to be totally cool, you can't show people how you feel. You have to maintain a completely nonchalant, "I couldn't care less about anything" look on your face.

You are having a totally awesome day and life is great—but don't smile. That's not *cool.*

You just flunked a midterm and found out that you've been laid off at work—but don't look sad. That's not *cool.*

If you walk by someone at school in whom you are really interested and just give him a cool, unexpressive look coupled with a quick "Howya doin'?" your chances of getting a date with him are remote. The message you just sent is that you are about as excited to talk to him as you'd be to talk to the wall.

Think about it. You just gave him the same amount of attention you would give the wall. "Howya doin', floor? Howya doin', wall? Howya doin', person?" It all says you aren't interested.

There's a time to be cool in a relationship and a time not to be cool. The beginning, when you are trying to get someone's attention, is definitely the time *not* to be cool.

You must let him know without a doubt that you are interested. The message must get through loud and clear. Most people won't ask you out if there's any chance you will say no. Rather than be turned down, they simply won't ask.

So how do you let someone know you are interested?

The first thing you must do is look at him. Eyes say everything. Eyes can say, *You have my undivided attention, and I want to talk to you.*

Next, you smile. A smile says, *You make me happy. I want to be around you.*

Now, speak to him. Always say something positive that will build his or her self-esteem. "Hey, Tiffany, you're looking great today," or "I saw your game Friday, and you were terrific!"

Be careful that the compliment you pay is sincere. People can see right through a phony. Also, be careful that your compliment is not sexually oriented. Though you may have said something to be cute or complimentary, it may come through as being too sexy, disrespectful, or overly aggressive.

If you have carefully followed these steps and the individual still doesn't get the message, then just hit him over the head with your notebook and say, "Hey, dummy, I like you. Ask me out, and I will say yes."

Just kidding!

With a warm smile, a glimmer in your eye, and a sincere compliment, the message can't help but get through. If your prospective date has the same feelings or interest, there's a good chance you'll be hearing from him soon.

What if you don't hear from him? Don't worry about it. Nothing is worse than a forced relationship. Don't ask someone out who you know doesn't like you or doesn't want to go out with you. The date will be disastrous. If you have given the person all the right signs and he simply doesn't respond, just let it go. He has lost out on the opportunity to have one of the greatest dates of his life. He loses, not you. There are plenty of other fish in the sea.

Let's say that you've given him all the right signs and he *is* interested. You will know because he will smile back at you while he looks straight into your eyes and thanks you for your compliment. Also, you will suddenly feel your heart speed up about fifty beats per minute. This is a sure sign!

Now to ask this person out.

If you're a guy, you need to know that women like men who are confident and know where they are going in life. For your first couple of dates, since you are the one who is doing the asking and you are paying, you make the decision as to where you go and what you do. Call her with "the plan."

"Hi, Becky. This is Joe Cool. How are ya? Great. I'd like to catch [name a great flick you want to see] Friday night. Would you like to go?"

Notice that you don't ask her if she has seen the movie. Girls usually won't lie, and if they have seen it, they will tell you the truth. What guys don't understand is that even if she has seen the film three or four times, it doesn't matter to her. She hasn't seen it with you, and that makes all the difference in the world. She just wants to be with you. The movie is irrelevant.

Uh-oh! What if the film you've been invited to is R-rated, and you have chosen not to see R-rated or vulgar movies? Just explain to your date that you are really excited to have the chance to go out with him but that you would really rather not see that particular film. Make another suggestion, and see what happens. Chances are he just wants to be with you, too, and the choice of movie doesn't really matter.

If he presses you about seeing that film, however, don't be afraid to stand up for your convictions. People usually admire and respect those who stand up for what they believe in, even if they don't agree.

Before you end your call, guys, make sure your date knows the day and time you'll be picking her up. If you don't know where she lives, get her address and instructions on how to get there. Better to ask than to show up thirty minutes late because you got lost.

Last of all, tell her you are really looking forward to seeing her. She will be so excited she won't sleep for days!

If you are planning something informal or casual, ask your date three to five days in advance. This shows you are looking ahead and planning for a fun activity.

For formal dates, ask one or preferably two weeks in advance. This allows time for shopping for a new dress or renting a tuxedo, ordering flowers, and making financial arrangements.

Don't ask a date out the day of or the night before. This shows that you don't plan ahead, that the date is just a last-minute afterthought, or that you couldn't get another date.

In some cases, however, you may decide to get a date at the last minute and do something with a group of friends. Ask someone you know and have been out with before. Explain that you and your friends just got this crazy idea to get together and that you would like to know if he or she wants to go with you.

If you are a girl and it's girls' choice, do *not* call the guy to ask him out. Though it may seem a little old-fashioned, ladies still don't call men.

You've got to be kidding! is probably going through your mind right now, and *Why not?*

Though times and customs may change, I have found that some things never do. Men like to be men. By their nature they are more aggressive and protective, and they love to take care of and protect women. Calling a date seems to be a more masculine thing to do.

"Hello, Joe Cool, this is Jenny. Do you wanna go out Friday night?"

See what I mean? It doesn't seem very feminine.

A much better way to ask a guy out would be to ask in a creative way. There are tons of creative ways to ask a date out and tons of creative dates. We will discuss these ideas in our chapter on creative dating. (I am only using a movie date as an example in this chapter because it is a very common—though not very creative—date.)

Another reason for girls not to call guys is that it

annoys a guy's sense of independence. He may tell you he wants you to call, but when it comes down to it, he really doesn't.

For example, a girl has been dating a guy for a couple of months, and he says, "Hey, Carol, why don't you ever call me? I call you all the time, but you never call me."

Reluctantly the girl says, "Well, OK."

The first time she calls the guy, he is thrilled. Why shouldn't he be? It's obvious now that she really likes him. The next time she calls, though, he's not quite as excited, and he wonders what she wants. The next time, not only is he not excited but he begins to wonder if she's checking up on him or something.

You see, what seemed like a good idea is now beginning to be a bother.

Young ladies simply don't call young men.

Let the guys be the pursuers. Be a challenge for them. They love the chase. There's an old saying that is still applicable today: "Guy chases girl till she catches him." Think about it. A smart young lady will understand this completely.

So what do you do if a guy asks you to call him?

Just tell him you don't call guys. Make a joke and say you have a female hand and that it only dials female phone numbers. If he presses the issue, tell him you just don't feel comfortable calling guys. It's not just him. You don't call any guys. Even if the young man disagrees with your policy, he'll find comfort in knowing that though you may not be calling him, you aren't calling other guys, either.

Accepting a date is easy to do. You just say in an excited voice, "Yes, I would love to_____(filling in the blank with whatever the date is going to be).

Major problem, however: What if you really want to go out with him but you already have plans? How do you let him know you like him and want him to ask again?

Tell him, "Oh, I would love to _____ but I already have plans for that night. Do you think we could go the next night instead?"

This will let him know you are definitely interested. The person and the activity are great, but the day is not.

If he says the day you suggested is not good for him, apologize and tell him how sorry you are that it didn't work out for that weekend. Tell him you really would like to get together another time and to please call again.

Major problem II: What if you don't want to go out with him? You have nothing in common, or you know that he doesn't have the same moral values and convictions you do. Perhaps you know absolutely nothing about this person other than his name.

It is very unwise to date people without knowing a little something about who they are and their character. Not only is it unwise, but it can be dangerous. Too often the intentions of one person might not be congruent with the intentions of the other.

What, then, is the polite way to turn the date down?

The best way is to be kind. In a nice but not excited tone of voice, tell him you are sorry but you already have plans. (Your plans may be to wash your hair or help your younger sister with her homework. He doesn't have to know the specifics.) Then thank him for asking, and end the call as quickly as possible.

Sometimes a guy will call a second time just to make sure he didn't misunderstand your message or to see if perhaps you have changed your mind. If you still feel the same way, kindly make your excuse of being busy again, and end the call. Rarely will he call a third time.

It's not so much what you say in accepting or refusing a date but the tone in which you say it. If you sound really excited, he will know you are interested and will ask again. If you don't sound excited, he won't.

Dating Courtesies

Miracle! You have a date! You asked, they accepted, we're excited. But now, how to treat your date?

Start the date off right by being on time. Nothing is quite so annoying as to have your date tell you he will pick you up at seven, only to show up at seven-thirty. By the time you have been stewing for a half hour and worrying if you got the time wrong or if he has had an accident, you are not going to be very good company.

With the same respect in mind, you girls should be ready when your dates arrive to pick you up. You should be the ones to open the door, flash a big smile, and extend a warm hello. Don't let your parents open the door. It's terrifying for a guy to have some strange adult open the door as he is standing there wondering if he even has the right house. If you aren't ready, it's even worse to have your date sit alone in your living room with your parents and try to carry on an interesting conversation.

Do have your date come inside and meet your parents. Every loving parent is concerned about whom their youth are spending time with. They want to meet your friends and get to know them a little.

Remember from chapter 1 how to meet people?

Straighten your back, look your date's father straight in the eye, smile, and say, "How do you do, Mr. Brown? It's a pleasure to meet you, sir."

If you do this, your date's father will immediately have a cardiac arrest. He will be completely shocked at the way you present yourself and the class that you project. Chances are he will be thinking to himself, *Not only can my daughter go out with this young man, she can marry him!* All parents want their children to have classy friends.

The last thing you do before leaving your house is to tell your parents where you will be for the evening. You don't have to give addresses or phone numbers, but give them an idea of where you will be. "Mom, we are going to the show to see _____ and then to Pizza Hut to eat with some friends. See you later." This is a courtesy to your parents so they will know where to find you in case of an emergency.

This very thing happened to me while dating. My father was in a terrible automobile accident out of town in which he was critically injured. Because my mother knew exactly where I was, she sent for me, and we were with him in a matter of a few short hours.

What about curfew?

Curfew is a very misunderstood part of dating. Most youth think curfew is the time when you have to come home. Wrong! The time to come home is when your date is over. Curfew simply means that your date needs to be over by that particular time at the latest.

Young people often don't get into trouble during their dates, but rather, after their date is over, when there's nothing planned to do until curfew. It is this period of time that can be dangerous.

Every family is different when it comes to rules and curfews. Just know that if your parents set early curfews, they are extremely interested in your happiness and welfare. They want you to have fun and enjoy yourself, but not at the risk of making mistakes that can change your life forever.

Now that your parents know where you are going, say something like this: "Good-bye. I love you. See you later." (Parents love to hear you say you love them!)

At last we're off. But wait. Now is the most important time we will ever have on our date. You see, the time from when we leave our home until we reach the car is when we set the tone for the date. We actually let our date know how we want to be treated.

I feel the young woman should set the example at this point. She should let the guy know how she wants to be treated.

I have found young men to be extremely accommodating. If a girl wants to be treated like a lady, he will treat her with that respect. But if she acts like one of the guys by cruising up to the car, opening the door for herself, and jumping in, he will assume she wants to be treated like one of the guys.

So how does a girl let a guy know that she wants to be treated like a lady? Tell him verbally, right?

"Joe Cool, I just thought you ought to know before we go out tonight that I'm a lady. I expect you to open car doors for me and take me to nice places. Do you have any questions?"

If you said that, your date would most likely respond with, "Yeah, I have two questions. Who's this weird woman I'm with, and where is my real date?"

Obviously, it can't be a verbal communication but a nonverbal one—one that will clearly let your date know how you want to be treated.

The best way for a girl to get this message across is to slip her fingertips gently through the arm of her date and rest them on his forearm. Make sure you never touch him between his elbow and his shoulder. Men have a natural tendency to flex their biceps when they are touched. It's a sort of "Hey, feel that muscle that's going to protect you" sign.

Occasionally when you do this, your date won't know what's happening and will go into total shock. He will say to himself, *I think there's something on my forearm. I think it's a hand.* Stunned, he will put his hand into his pocket and hope that maybe it will go away.

Don't remove your hand. As you walk to his car in this manner, it will automatically place you in a position for him to open the car door. After all, you are attached to him. He's not going to say "Hop in, honey" when he is right there at the door.

A guy who is used to dating "ladies" will know exactly what to do. The minute he feels those fingertips over his forearm, he will immediately bring his hand slowly up to or just slightly below his belt buckle. Along with this, his shoulders will rise slightly. This is a nonverbal statement back that says, "It's OK, little lady. You are out with a gentleman."

Sometimes girls will not know how to set the tone for the date. In that case, the young man should take over.

24

Let her know that she is out with one classy guy and that you expect her to act like a lady.

The nonverbal way to do this is simple. You don't have to look at her or say anything. As you walk her to the car, with her on your right, take your left hand and slip it into her left hand. Now place her hand onto your right forearm as you continue walking.

Your date will absolutely melt. She will be shocked at the fact that there are still gentlemen in this world who live and breathe and that she is lucky enough to be out with one of them.

When you reach the car door, the young lady should draw her hand away from her date. She should then step behind him and over a step or two to his left side. This will allow him room to open the door without bumping the door straight into her body (which could be very painful, I might add).

If the young lady does not move out of the way, it is the responsibility of the young man to move her. Guys, this is done by slipping your left hand through her left hand again and gently pulling her directly in front of you and to your left. Not only does this enable you to open the door freely, but you have again impressed her with your ability to take charge. Women *love* that!

To get into the car, a young lady may do one of two things: She may place her hips into the front seat and then draw both feet in at the same time, or she may place her left foot first on the front floorboard and quickly put her knees together as she draws in her right leg and sits down.

Young ladies should always remember that one of the basic rules in being a lady is that you always keep your knees together, and your ankles together, too, when possible. This applies no matter what kind of clothes you are wearing.

As soon as the door is closed, slant your knees toward your date and turn your body slightly toward him. This will help him feel more comfortable when he gets

25

into the car because you will be in good conversation position.

Your date has just extended a nice courtesy to you by opening your door. Return the favor by unlocking his door or by removing anything that may be in his way.

When you arrive at your destination, don't be in a hurry to get out of the car. Probably the number one reason men don't open car doors for women is that the women don't give them the opportunity. By the time they get out of the car and come around to catch the door, the woman has already gotten out and is halfway to the ticket booth. Slow down, ladies. Allow the men time to be the gentlemen they really are.

Uh-oh! What if he forgets the door? What if he takes off for the theater and leaves you sitting in the car? Don't worry. Sooner or later it will dawn on him that he is missing something—namely, his date.

What should you do when this happens? Sit there and wait, right? How about honking the horn? That should be a clue!

The answer is both yes and no. Yes, you do wait, but don't just sit there with your nose in the air expecting him to open the door, or, worse, honk the horn and let the whole world know he forgot.

One thing women sometimes forget is that there is only one reason men do nice things for women. It's not because Mother says it's the thing to do or because Vivian Cline says it's the proper way to act. The only reason a young man extends these courtesies to a young lady is that *he* wants to. It's the responsibility of the young lady to help create the right feelings and situations so he will want to do these things.

Always make your date look good. Compliment him. Cover for him if he makes a social mistake. He forgot the door, so make it look as though you didn't even notice. Quickly get busy going through your purse or resetting your watch. Fix the buckle on your shoe that has no buckle! The point is to cover for him. The minute he discovers that you are still in the car, he will rush back to get the door. How relieved he will be when he suspects that you were so busy doing something else you didn't even notice the delay.

If you need help in getting out of his car because you are wearing a formal or because his vehicle is difficult to get out of, ask for it. Men love to be of assistance if you really need help, but not if you are just acting helpless. Simply extend your hand to your date and say, "Steve, would you give me a hand, please?" He will respond by taking your hand and pulling you gently out of the car.

Never extend your hand to the young man with your wrist bent and your pinkie finger extended. This looks like a little doggie paw. It gives the impression that you are trying to be prissy, and men hate that.

Young ladies need to be aware that men do love women who are feminine but do not like women who act prissy. What's the difference? Being feminine is a natural and graceful way to act. Because you are calm and confident with yourself, it puts the man at ease. Being prissy, on the other hand, is exaggerating. It is overemphasizing every move and action. It looks phony.

Problem! Say this is a double or group date, and your date is not driving. The car you are going in is a two-door, not a four-door, and you have to get into the back-seat. How do you do that gracefully?

It's simple, right? When he opens the door and pulls the front seat back, you just bend over and dive in.

Wrong!

There's a major difference between a man's hips and a woman's. (You knew that already, didn't you?) A man's hips are perfectly straight. A lady's hips, on the other hand, are curved. When a lady bends over, the curve has a tendency to get much larger or curvier. As she bends over with her head in the car, there is only one thing exposed, and it looks twice as big as normal.

The young man is now left in a very awkward position. If he looks down at the woman's hips, he will be embarrassed for her. In an effort not to draw attention to this problem, he will typically look up and check the weather or glance at his watch and check the time. This buys the young lady enough time to quickly get into the car.

Pay close attention, young ladies, because there's a much better way to get into the backseat of a car gracefully. It's called "parallel parking."

That's right. You just parallel park yourself into the car. It's really very easy. As the door is opened for you, turn your body so that it's facing the same direction as the car. Your body will actually be parallel to the car. Now take your left foot and place it onto the backseat floorboard. Quickly touch your left knee with your right as you begin to slip your hips into the backseat. Your head will be pulled into the car as your hips touch the seat. The last thing to enter will be your right leg and foot. Draw them in slowly. (This same process works when you get into the left side of the car. Just do the same as above, except you will put the right foot in first and the left foot last.)

As your date watches this well-skilled maneuver, he will be most impressed. You will probably be the first date he ever had who actually "slithered" into the backseat of a car.

To get out of the car, you do just the opposite. Always exit on the same side your date exits. He will get out first and be ready to assist you if you need help. Place your right foot onto the pavement. Your left foot will remain on the backseat floorboard with your knees together. At this time you have to make a decision—you may either grab hold of the door and pull yourself out, or you can ask your cute date for some help. Which would you rather do? (Are you kidding? You get to hold his hand for a minute!)

Now reach your hand toward your date as you would to any friend and say, "Sam, would you mind giving me a hand, please?" He will be delighted to assist you, because it is obvious that you need help.

As you put your hand into his, he will gently pull you from the backseat of the car. Take your left leg out of the car last and cross it over slightly in front of the right leg. This will form a soft line at the hip, which is very figure-flattering.

This entire procedure has taken a couple of seconds, and your hand has been in his the whole time. If you really like your date a lot, let him know it. Squeeze his hand gently as you look into his eyes with a smile; then pull away softly, saying, "Thank you."

Your date will go bananas! He will be thinking to himself, *Not only are you welcome, little lady, but I will be happy to help you any ole time!*

What about conversation in the car while you're on your way? This can be an enjoyable or an uncomfortable time, depending on whether you know how to keep the conversation ball going back and forth.

The secret to a successful conversation is to not ask questions that can be answered by "yes" or "no."

For example, don't say, "John, I understand that you are on your school's basketball team. Is that right?"
Answer: "Yes."
Question: "So you really like to play basketball?"
Answer: "Yes."
Question: "Have you played for very long?"

29

Answer: "No."

Can you see where this conversation is going? Nowhere fast! The conversation ball is not being returned. Always ask questions that require thoughtful answers.

For example, you might say, "John, I understand that you are on your school's basketball team. That's great. Tell me, what do you enjoy most about playing basketball?"

Answer: "Yes."

Wrong! He won't say "yes" but will think about the question for a minute and tell you why he likes the sport. After he gives the answer, either he can return the conversation ball by asking you a question or else you can make a comment about his answer and continue to develop the conversation.

Don't hog the conversation by talking about yourself the entire time. A big mistake people sometimes make is to open their lives like a book and proceed to tell everything that has happened to them from birth until that very night!

What makes a book interesting is to read one chapter at a time and then enjoy and savor it. Get to know someone a little at a time. That way they will look forward to being with you again. You will be exciting to them, just like a new chapter in a book.

Another point to remember in developing a conversation is to try to find a common thread that interests you both. Continue asking questions about various subjects until you find one you both like.

Common topics of interest are school, sports, music, movies, and cars. Make sure you focus on the things that you have in common and not your differences. This will help keep things on a positive note.

Ending the Date

For most teens, ending the date seems to be the most difficult part. Parents tell you not to do this and not to do that, but no one ever seems to tell you what you should do.

The end of the date is important because it will be remembered the most. A good date and a good speech are similar—you need a good beginning and a great ending for both. What happens or is said in the middle is rarely the part that is remembered.

In deciding how you will end your date, it's helpful to know a little something about how the opposite sex thinks and feels. This will help you understand them better.

When a young man walks a young lady to her front door, numerous things flood his mind. He thinks about the great time he had with her and how different she is from other girls. He reflects back on how she set the tone for the date by putting her fingertips on his forearm, and how she all but glided into the car when he opened the door.

He remembers all the nice things she said about him and how she made him feel so special. The smile on her face and the gentle squeeze of his hand when she said, "Thank you." He has had one of the best dates of his life, but now he has to say good night, and he doesn't want to make a mistake.

Quickly he considers his options and his feelings. His first impulse is to sweep her into his arms and plant one on the "ole smackeroo." He knows how classy she is, however. If he does that, she may slap his face (with class, of course!).

On the other hand, if he doesn't at least attempt to kiss her good night, she may think he's a mama's boy who doesn't know how to handle himself with women—and he does.

By this time you are at the door. Now, what to do!

At the same time the young man is having this flood of thoughts, the young lady is reminiscing too. What a wonderful evening she's just had! She's been treated like a queen. How surprised she was when he placed her fingertips on his forearm and escorted her to the car. Not one door did she have to open. His smile just melted her, and he made her feel as though she was the most important thing in the whole world. How lucky she was to go out with such a great guy! How would she ever say good night in just the right way?

Quickly she considers her options and her feelings. Her first impulse would be to let him kiss her. It would probably be ecstasy. Wait! What would he think of her? He would probably wonder if she lets every guy who takes her out kiss her good night, and she doesn't. She's not that kind of girl. On the other hand, if she doesn't let him kiss her, he might think she doesn't like him, or worse—that she's a prude.

By now you are at the door. What *do* you do?

You have probably been able to identify with some of the feelings I've just discussed. You can also foresee that there is going to be a major problem at the front door. It's called a stalemate. It goes something like this:

"Well, Walt, I sure had a good time tonight."

"Yeah, I did too."

"The movie was really great."

"Yeah, it was really great."

"And the pizza was the best I think I've ever had."

"Yeah, it was super."

"Well, thanks again." She stands there silently looking at the porch steps.

"You're welcome." He stands there silently looking around and evaluating the situation.

Stop here for a minute, and put yourself in the place of the guy. You are at the front door of your date's house. She isn't saying anything. You aren't saying anything. Your masculinity is now being questioned. What would you do?

Someone has to break the stalemate. Chances are you would probably just lean over and plunk one on her. After all, she's standing there waiting for something to happen, and you are certainly no mama's boy!

No! Stop! There is a better way.

Just as I stated earlier—that I believe it's the responsibility of the young lady to set the tone for the date—I also believe it's the responsibility of the young lady to end the date.

Young ladies, don't put the guys into such an awkward predicament. They have enough pressures in their lives, and they don't need any more. Make the door scene an easy one. You take the initiative to end the date.

Tell him what a wonderful time you had and how much you enjoyed the date. Maybe even suggest that you get together again sometime, especially if you really like him. Now do something really hard. Put your hand on the doorknob and turn it. Push the door open, and walk slowly inside. Turn around, and look at your date one more time. Smile at him, or maybe even give him a little wink as you tell him one last time, "Thanks again. Good night!"

You cannot believe how relieved the young man will be to have the door scene be so comfortable. He will know what a great time you had, because you told him. You also suggested that maybe you could go out again sometime. This is a sure sign that you are interested. All the way back to the car he will be thinking that he has very possibly had one of the best dates of his life.

What about a good-night kiss? Is there anything wrong with a little kiss on the lips at the front door?

That depends on a lot of things.

First of all, never, never, never kiss on the first date. Whatever you do on the first date sets the precedent for all your following dates with that person. If you kissed on the first date, is there any question whether you will kiss on the next date? Why stop a good thing, right?

Second, remember that whatever you do, your date will assume that you do that with all your dates. If you kiss on the first date, he will wonder if you let all your dates kiss you. (He may think you have hot lips or something!)

Third, a kiss is like the seasoning of a recipe. When you add a little spice every now and then, it makes the recipe taste great. But if you dump the whole can of spice in, it will surely ruin the food.

It's important to remember that a kiss is a token of one's affection. Kisses should be saved for people with whom we have developed sincere and meaningful relationships. They should never be considered a normal part of the date. A kiss should also be a mutual expression of affection. Both parties should be willing. Never force those feelings. When the time is right, you will know.

Last of all, a kiss starts the wheels in motion to a physical relationship with that person. Intimate relationships should be reserved for marriage, and you will want to make sure that you don't do anything that would push you too far in that direction before marriage.

Know yourself well. Decide now how you will behave in situations where your values may be compromised. Never allow others to push you away from what you know is right.

Well, there you have it—the recipe for a fantastic date from start to finish. It's really quite simple. Let the person you'd like to date know that you are interested. Be warm and friendly. While on your date, treat him or her with respect and kindness, just the way you would like to be treated. And last of all, close the date in a comfortable way by expressing your thanks with no strings attached.

You may be thinking about now that these ideas are great if you're on a date with someone you really like, but what if you're with someone you aren't really interested in? I understand completely, because this very thing happened to me.

When I was a freshman in college, my cousin Julaine phoned me one day. She said her boyfriend, Bob, had a good friend from high school who was passing through town, and she wondered if I would go out with him on a triple date.

As you well know, this is called a blind date. My first response was the typical "What does this guy look like?"

Julaine said she didn't know because she had never met him before. She said that Bob had told her he was a really nice guy in high school. Besides, it was a group date with a third couple, so I would never be alone with him.

My next question was, "What is he studying in college?"

She told me he was a pre-medical student, so I knew that at least we would be able to have some interesting conversation. Since I owed my cousin a favor, I said OK.

The night of my date came. I was upstairs in my bedroom putting the finishing touches on my hair when the door to my bedroom burst open. There stood my roommate with the biggest smile on her face.

"Vivian," she said with great enthusiasm, "you lucked out. He's gorgeous."

I couldn't believe my good fortune. My first good-looking blind date. I quickly fluffed up my hair and grabbed my favorite perfume bottle for a little extra dash (pssssssssssssssssssssssssss, five minutes later!) of fragrance.

My roommate told me that my date was in the kitchen getting a drink of water. Down the stairs I bounced with great eagerness to meet this incredible hunk. But there in the kitchen, to my great astonishment, was Bob.

Shock ran through my body as I tried to pull myself together. I looked at Bob. He smiled, said hello, and pointed into the living room, saying, "I'd like you to meet an old friend of mine."

With great hesitation I looked into the living room, and there he stood. Let's just say he was . . . unique, and *definitely* not my type. Suddenly I was faced with a tremendous decision—I could put my nose up in the air and get the evening over with as quickly as possible, or I could do something that my mother taught me as a little girl growing up in the South. "Sometimes, darlin'," she would say, "the best thing to do is just grin and bear it."

I looked at my cousin. It wasn't her fault I had lucked out with this date. If I acted rude to him it would just make everyone else miserable too. Or I could do something else that was a lot tougher: I could swallow my pride and, like Mother said, "Grin and bear it." I decided to take my mother's advice.

With all the composure I could muster, I looked into the living room and, pretending that he was Prince Charming, put a big smile on my face and said, "Well, hello, John. It's a pleasure to meet you."

A sudden sense of relief filled the room as everyone realized that the evening would be OK.

The next morning, at about ten o'clock, I received a phone call. You will never believe who called me. My date, right? Wrong! He was on his way home to California. Bob, right? Wrong! My cousin had that all sewn up.

Now your mind is starting to strain. Remember, I said this was a triple date. I didn't tell you anything about the third couple, though, did I?

The young man was extremely attractive. He had dark, neat, combed hair and wore dress slacks with a crease down the front and a smooth leather jacket. His smile was awesome, and he drove a brand-new custom-made Porsche with leather interior. I took one look at him and thought, *Yes!*

His date was a tall, beautiful blond with baby blue eyes, pearly white teeth, and a figure to die for. I took one look at her and thought, *Forget it!*

I had hardly said more than two words to either of them the whole evening, and here he was on the other end of the phone.

"Hello, Vivian, this is Pete. How are you?"

My heart almost stopped. I couldn't believe this cool guy was calling me!

"Fine," I said, trying to contain my excitement. "How are you?"

"Great. I just wanted to call and thank you for what you did last night."

I was surprised. "What do you mean?"

"Well," he said, "it was obvious to everyone that you didn't get paired up with your ideal date. But you handled yourself in a way that made everyone feel comfortable about it. That's the kind of girl I like to take out. Do you have any plans for this weekend?"

You better believe I didn't have any plans for that weekend! I ended up dating this young man for two years. Though the "love bug" never bit, we became good dating friends.

The moral of this story is simple: Instead of trying to find the perfect date, we need to be more concerned with *becoming* the best date. Instead of thinking of ourselves first and what people can do to please us, we need to be more aware of others and their wants and needs. If you do this, I think you will find, as I did, that you will come out on top every time.

If you follow the simple guidelines in this chapter, your circle of dating friends will likely expand. The friendships you establish will be dear and long lasting. Instead of looking for the perfect date, become the perfect date, and chances are the two of you will eventually meet!

CHAPTER FOUR

THE ART
OF DINING

Few things can be so enjoyable or so miserable as eating a meal with others. It can be tremendously enjoyable if we are comfortable with our dining skills, because we can concentrate on our dinner companions and our conversation with them. It is terribly uncomfortable, however, if we don't know how to eat correctly. We then tend to be nervous and worry about whether we are doing the right thing, instead of enjoying the food and the good company. Sometimes we even let the food go back into the kitchen because we aren't quite sure how to eat it. Rather than embarrass ourselves, we would go hungry!

This chapter is dedicated to teaching basic dining skills that are applicable all the time, whether the meal is formal or not.

I would like to start by telling you why I enjoy teaching dining skills. You might think that I am one of those extremely proper people who was raised with a silver spoon in her mouth and therefore grew up knowing all the right things to do. Wrong!

39

I grew up in a small town in the central part of Georgia. It was a rural community similar to Mayberry on the television series *The Andy Griffith Show.* Everyone there knew everyone else, and it was a very simple town. Since my parents were both Southerners, I grew up eating traditional Southern foods such as turnip greens, black-eyed peas, corn bread, and buttermilk. I naturally assumed that the rest of the world did too.

When I turned fourteen, my father lost his job and we had to move to Atlanta so he could find employment. I was excited and yet terrified of moving to the big city.

After settling into school, I quickly befriended a young lady by the name of Vicky. Vicky was from a very well-to-do family. One day she invited me to sleep over, and with the permission of my parents, I decided to accept.

I knew I was in big trouble when she picked me up at my modest home in a fancy car. I knew that I was in bigger trouble when we drove up to her house and it had white pillars in front. And I knew that I was dead in the water when I met her mother. She was a banking executive and was dressed in a business suit, wore her hair up in a French twist, and had cocktails before dinner.

Knowing full well that I was what you might call a "country bumpkin," I decided to try to not make a fool of myself. My thoughts quickly wandered to dinner and whether I would know how to eat what they were serving. I asked Vicky what we were having, and she said fried shrimp. Panic suddenly ran through my body. I had seen shrimp on television but had never eaten any. After being seated at the table, I noticed that everyone picked up their linen dinner napkins and placed them in their laps. I had never seen a cloth napkin. We used napkins at my house, but they were made of paper, and sometimes we even used paper towels. I proceeded to do the same with an air of "Oh yes, we do this at my house, too."

I needed to buy some time so I could see how the others ate the shrimp. I picked up my water goblet and started to sip slowly as I watched the mother out of the corner of my eye. After all, mothers never made mistakes!

I noticed that she picked up the fried shrimp with her fingers, dipped it into this red stuff, and put it into her mouth.

No problem, I thought with relief. *This is simple. You just dip the shrimp into that red stuff and eat it.*

I was eager now to exhibit my newly learned skill.

Gently I picked up my shrimp, dipped it into my cocktail sauce, and popped it into my mouth. Suddenly, as I began to chew, Vicky said with astonishment, "Gross me out, you eat the tails?"

Tails! There was a tail on that thing? I had a *tail* in my mouth? I was now in total shock as every ounce of blood in my body quickly rushed to my head and I turned red with embarrassment.

Instantly Vicky's mother, being the true lady that she was, covered for me. "Yes, Vicky," she said, looking sternly at her daughter, "some people enjoy the entire shrimp."

Never have I been so grateful for a kind mother who quickly saved me from the height of embarrassment. Right then and there I promised myself that never again would I subject myself to such humiliation. I would read, I would take classes and study, I would do whatever was needed to learn the social skills necessary to present myself well in public.

Unfortunately, as a youth I thought the way to have class was to be rich. I didn't realize that owning china, crystal, and silver did not bring you class, but the skill with which to use them did. You can have just as much class with Tupperware and Melmac as with any fancy dishes. Class is not a purchasable commodity but a skill that anyone who will just take the time can learn. So let's learn how to be classy while we eat!

There are several basic rules to remember that will help you in almost any dining situation. Because dining at a restaurant is the most common concern, we will pretend we are going to a nice restaurant for dinner.

When you enter the restaurant, a maitre d' or hostess will ask you how many are in your party. If you are on a date, the gentleman should give the correct number. If you are with a group of friends, you need to designate someone in your group to be in charge and respond.

A waiter or hostess will show you to your table. The lady or ladies should follow the waiter and the men follow the ladies as you are escorted to your table. Sometimes, if it is a single couple, the waiter will seat the lady and assist the gentleman as well. If there is more than one couple, each gentleman should be responsible for helping his date be seated and should then seat himself. In a group of friends, the gentlemen should offer to assist the ladies out of courtesy, even though it's not a date.

The best seating arrangement is to always alternate males with females at a round table. This ensures a good mixture of conversation. A single couple should sit across from each other. Double dates should sit next to their dates and across the table from the opposite sex. If girl faces girl and guy faces guy, the conversation has a tendency to split up into girl talk and guy talk. Again, sitting across the table from opposites will encourage a mixture of conversation.

After you are seated, immediately pick up your dinner napkin and place it on your lap. Do this before you look at your menu or take a drink of water.

Make sure your napkin is folded in half with the fold away from you. This is so you can open your napkin, blot your lips, and replace the napkin in the same folded position. Because the napkin is back in a closed position, no one can see the oil or tiny crumbs it may contain.

Now it's time to order. If you are paying for yourself, choose whatever you would like. If you are with a date or someone else who is paying, please be considerate of his or her finances.

The person who is paying should offer suggestions about what to order. If this doesn't happen, a good way to get him or her to offer a suggestion would be to say, "Gee,

THE ART OF DINING

what sounds good?" or "What are you in the mood to eat tonight?" If you have never eaten at the restaurant, say, "I've never eaten here before. What would you suggest?"

Everyone has different tastes, and what may be wonderful to one person may be gross to another. Never say anything negative about a food that is suggested. You will be sure to offend someone. If it is not to your liking, simply say, "That sounds good, but I think I will have _____" and then order something comparable in price.

The traditional way of ordering if a couple is on a date is for the lady to give her order to her date and then he gives it to the waiter. I am a very curious person and will sometimes research rules that I don't understand. Women are certainly capable of ordering for themselves, so why give the order to the man and let him relay the message?

In my research, I learned that back in the old days when women wore long dresses, women of fine upbringing were encouraged not to speak with men to whom they had not been properly introduced. Thus, the lady gave her order to her date with whom she was properly acquainted, and he gave it to the stranger.

Customs change. It is no longer unacceptable for women to speak to someone to whom they have not been introduced. A lady may now give her order directly to the waiter. When on a double or group date, this is probably the easiest way. However, when you are on a single date I think it shows respect for your date to allow him the privilege of ordering for you. Either way is correct.

When it is a girls' choice date, the young lady should give her date an adequate sum of money to cover the meal when he picks her up. If she picks him up, she should ask him to handle the money for her when they get in the car. This makes the guy feel more comfortable. Guys don't wear a sign on them that says, "This is a girls' choice date. She's paying." When he handles the money, it looks like a normal date. If the girl pays, it looks like he is a cheap date!

Dutch treat dates are informal dates in which each person pays for himself. In this case, ask the waiter for separate checks before you order.

If there is no food on the table, it's permissible to place your elbows on the table with your hands together in a propped-up fashion. When there is food on the table, however, elbows on the table are taboo.

At last, your food has arrived. No one should begin eating until everyone at the table has been served. An exception to this is if you are at someone's home and the hostess asks you to go ahead and begin your meal without her. The only other exception is when you are at a banquet table that seats many people. In that case, wait to begin eating until the people with whom you came have been served. Then you may go ahead of the others at the table and begin eating.

Many entrees, or main courses, include a soup, salad, or both; your main meal; and a house dessert for one price. Check your menu carefully to make sure this is the case. If your menu says "a la carte" it means you will be charged separately for each item you order. This can add up to a lot of money, so be prepared.

Our soup has now been served.

Unless you order something that is served with a separate eating utensil, you will find your utensil on the table. A basic rule of thumb is to start from the outside pieces of silverware and work your way in toward your plate. Your forks will be to the left side of the plate, and your spoons will be to the right. The largest spoon will be your soup spoon.

Pick up the soup spoon and hold it as you would a pencil, between your index and middle finger and braced by your thumb. Never hold your silver in a shovel position. A shovel position is when you wrap all your fingers around the utensil in a fist and your thumb is either pressed against the utensil or tucked under the fist.

With the spoon held in the correct position, you may now dip it into the soup in a direction away from you. If you need to tip the spoon onto the outside edge of the bowl so you won't drip, then do so. If not, bring the spoon directly to the mouth. Clear or creamed soups may be sipped quietly from the edge of your spoon. Soups that are thick or contain chunks of food are placed in your mouth.

Never blow on your food to cool it. Either wait till it cools naturally or gently stir it around to hasten the process.

Another rule of thumb to remember is that once you pick up a piece of silverware, it never touches the table again. Why? Because it is soiled, and if you place it on the tablecloth you will soil the cloth.

When your soup is finished, place your spoon in the bowl with the handle against the outside edge. If your soup was served in a cup with a serving saucer under it, lay the spoon on the saucer next to the cup. Never put a spoon into a cup and leave it in an upright position. This makes it easy to knock over if your arm passes by.

If the soup was delicious, you may tip the bowl away from you in order to get the last bite. That is a compliment to the chef that you enjoyed it so much you had to finish every drop.

What if the soup was not delicious? What if it was terrible? Do you have to eat it anyway? The answer is a definite no! You are always obligated to at least taste a food. It's fun to try new things. But if you find it is not to your liking, you don't have to finish it.

Don't announce to the others at your table that you don't like your soup. When asked how you liked it, say, "It

45

was nice but very different than I had expected." This allows others to enjoy their soup without feeling that you think they have bad taste.

Next comes the salad. House salads usually consist of half a head of lettuce with one lonely cherry tomato set on top in all its glory.

Look to the far left of your plate and you will see a small fork and a large one. Remember the rule to choose the outside utensil first. This will be your small fork and is referred to as your salad fork. If the lettuce is not in bite-sized pieces and you need to cut it, do so first with your salad fork. A knife should be used only if the fork won't do the job.

Uh-oh! After you use your knife to cut the lettuce, where does the knife go? We know it can't touch the table again, right? Exactly! You're catching on.

After you use your knife, place it on the outside edge of your salad plate or bowl either in a horizontal or diagonal position. Always place the cutting edge or blade toward the center of the plate or bowl. You may also place your knife on your bread-and-butter plate if you prefer.

What about that lonely cherry tomato? What's the proper way to eat it?

First of all, never try to chase it with your fork. It runs marathons and will outrun you every time.

The best thing to do is to trap it. Take your fork in your left hand with the tines down and push the tomato against the knife that is being held against the plate by your right hand. Once the tomato is braced against the knife, pierce it with your fork and slice it in half, eating only one half at a time.

Never put the entire tomato in your mouth and begin to chew. You may find a mini nuclear explosion happening and tiny tomato seeds being expelled from your mouth with great force!

Now for the bread and butter. How do you eat it correctly?

You may have heard the expression, "Won't you break bread with me?" That's how you eat bread: Break off one piece at a time, and eat each piece in one bite.

What about butter?

Butter is usually served by the individual pat on a separate plate. Never put your butter directly onto your bread from the butter dish. Place your butter on your bread-and-butter plate, or, if you don't have one, on your dinner plate. Pass the butter on to others and then begin to butter your bread one piece at a time.

Always be careful to put only the amount of food into your mouth that can be chewed and swallowed in a short time. This way you can quickly answer a question that may be asked you while you are eating.

Can you talk with food in your mouth? Yes, if it's a short answer and your mouth isn't very full.

Soup and salad are done; now on to the main course.

Let's pretend that we are having prime rib. (Is this chapter making you hungry or what!) Two methods are considered correct for proper eating: The first is called the zigzag or American method, and the second is called the European or Continental method.

To eat meat using the American method, you pick up your dinner fork, which is the large fork to your left, with your left hand and your dinner knife with your right hand. The tines of the fork should be pointing down. Your index finger should be at the base on the back of your fork but not touching the portion that touches your food. The handle of your fork will be tucked under your hand and will rest at the inside base of your little finger. (See illustration.)

Now, cut your meat into two or three pieces. Put the knife down on the edge of the dinner plate in a diagonal or horizontal position with the blade facing the center. Change the fork from the left hand to the right hand, pierce the piece of meat, and place it in your mouth. Return the fork to the left hand, pick up the knife with the right hand, and start the procedure all over again.

The Continental style of eating is much simpler. Pick up your fork in your left hand and your knife in your right. Cut a piece of meat, pierce it with your fork still in your left hand, and put it into your mouth. This is a much better way to eat meat. You may also eat your vegetables with your fork in that position, or you may turn the fork over in the usual fashion.

If you have a hard time getting your vegetables onto the back of your fork, try mixing them with your potatoes. They will stick much better.

By the way, this is the only time it is permissible to mix your food. Nothing is worse to look at than a plate full of scrambled up meat and vegetables (unless, of course, it's a stir-fry).

I would like to add a little side note of interest here.

One day I was at my kitchen sink thinking about the way we eat. I wondered why we eat using the American style when the Continental style is so much more practical.

Suddenly, an idea dawned on me!

When the United States broke away from England back in 1776, we tried to be different. We wanted to break our English traditions and have American ones instead. It seems to me that because the English drank tea, we began drinking coffee. The English drove on the left side of the road, so we switched to the right side. They used the metric system of measure, so we developed another system. It appears we wanted to prove to England that we were different.

Well, I think that after some two-hundred-plus years of being different, we made our point. Because the Continental style of eating is so much easier, I find more and more people using it. Try it a few times and see how you like it. Either way of eating is considered correct, so use the one that is most comfortable for you.

Oh, is this prime rib good! We are doing a beautiful job of handling our fork and knife in the Continental method. Uh-oh! We put a piece of prime rib in our mouth, and as we begin to chew we make an incredible discovery. It's not meat—it's yucky fat and gristle.

Quickly our mind runs through ways of disposing of it.

First option: Can we swallow it? How large is it? It's huge. If we try to swallow it, we may throw up on our date. Not cool!

Second option: We could spit it out onto our plate. This would definitely gross out our date. Again, not cool!

Third option: The napkin trick. We will just bring our dinner napkin to our mouth as though we are going to blot our lips. Instead, we will place that piece of fat into the napkin and fold it over. No one will know what we have just done. Cool, huh? Everyone thought we were being classy by blotting our lips, and we were really hiding that hunk of fat.

Wrong! The problem with that method is that later during our dinner we may really need to blot our lips. We pick up the napkin, forgetting that we had placed that major wad of fat in it, and out drops the fat onto our nice clothes. Worse yet, it falls on the floor and the waiter steps on it and takes a slide.

Fourth option: Some of the traditional etiquette books suggest the proper thing to do is to take it out with the utensil in which it was placed.

Think about this option for a minute. If you are having dinner with someone and he brings an empty fork to his mouth, are you going to notice? Probably. You will wonder what he's going to do with the empty fork. Oh, gross. He's putting gunkies on it.

Think also about how you will get the fat onto the fork. If you try to drop it onto the fork, you may miss the fork and it will land in your lap. If you try to spear the fat, you will have to roll the fat forward to the front of your tongue and then stab it with your fork.

You now have it on your fork, but how do you get it off? You will either have to use another utensil for assistance or you will have to drag it across the edge of your plate and hope it slips off. Again, with all the attention it will bring to you—not cool!

Fifth (and best) option: Keep your chin level. Bring your thumb and index finger to your mouth. Remove the fat and place it onto your plate. Now quickly use your fork and cover it with peas, parsley, anything. Just don't let that ugly thing sit there and stare back at you.

A couple of things to remember when using this method are, first, don't lower your head when you remove the fat. If you do, everyone will look to see what you are doing. (Gross, taking fat out!) And second, don't look someone straight into their eyes when you are removing it. Wait until your dinner companion takes a drink of water, cuts a piece of meat, or looks away for a moment. The point is to not draw attention to anything unpleasant.

This same method is best in removing small bones, pieces of shell, or anything that is solid and uncomfortable in your mouth.

After all this work of removing the fat from your mouth with total discretion, you are now thirsty. Time to take a sip of water or whatever you have chosen to drink.

Before you take a drink, always blot your lips with your napkin. Why? One good look into a glass that has been used without blotting the lips will give you the answer. There will either be little floaties or an oil slick on the surface of the beverage. Blotting first will remove any oil or particles of food that may be on your lips.

The best way to hold a water goblet is to take your fourth finger (next to your pinkie finger) and place it at the bottom of the bulb of the goblet and the top of the stem. Place your second and third finger against the lower part of the bulb with your fingertips and let your thumb tip brace the other side. The pinkie finger may lightly touch the stem or may extend slightly away from it.

Don't let your pinkie finger stick out to Timbuktu. This is an exaggerated look and comes across as prissy. And don't try to hide your pinkie by placing it on the other side of the stem. It's uncomfortable and looks strange.

A common mistake in holding the goblet is to hold it at the top or near the rim with the fingers close together and the thumb supporting the other side. This is commonly referred to as the "claw" method. As you lift your goblet to take a drink, your elbow will stick out and may hit your neighbor. Not only will this disturb your neighbor but it looks barbaric as well.

This same method is used when you have a glass. Hold it at the base, not the top, with the same finger position you used with the goblet.

What a wonderful meal! And you have looked like the epitome of class while using all your newly acquired dining skills.

But wait—you discover that you have a major problem you hadn't counted on. There's something stuck in the middle of your front teeth. It's half the prime rib!

Options again begin whirling through your head.

First option: Use your tongue to go across your teeth and possibly dislodge the meat. You try it, but nothing happens. You do it once more, but again, nothing happens.

Second option: Everyone does this, but few will admit it. You try to suck it back into your mouth between your teeth. Try as you may, it doesn't budge. You are beginning to think it may become a permanent part of your dental work.

Third option: The traditional etiquette books say to dislodge the imperfection with a toothpick. That might be a good option if you happen to be packing your own toothpicks. But what are the chances of that? What about a toothpick at your table? I have never seen a toothpick at the table in a classy restaurant. Even at an informal restaurant, you don't receive a toothpick until you have paid your bill. You could possibly ask for one, but the object here is to not draw attention to what you are trying to correct. If, however, by some small miracle you do find a toothpick, make sure that you cover it with the opposite hand as you draw it to your mouth. This will minimize the attention of what you are doing.

Fourth option (only use this option after you have already tried the first three with no success): I saw this done by a beautiful lady at a very formal dinner dance. She kept her chin level and drew her left hand to her mouth. With her fingers slightly separated she covered her lips. She took her right hand to her lips, and, with her pinkie fingernail hidden discreetly behind her left fingers, she quickly dislodged the imperfection.

If I hadn't been looking at her from across another table, I would have never seen her do it. I'm sure there were those who knew what she was doing, but she did it so quickly and with such class that no one cared.

The trick with this method is, first, keep the chin level. If you look down, everyone will look to see what you are doing. (Oh, gross, she's picking her teeth!)

Next, make sure the fingers on your left hand are covering your mouth and not your nose. If you cover your nose, what will people think? (I'm not even going to say!)

The last thing to remember is that you only get two tries to dislodge the imperfection. If you haven't removed it in those two tries, excuse yourself from the table and go to the restroom to pick your teeth. Don't sit there with your hands in that position picking your teeth half the night for all to see. Remember, the ultimate goal is to never draw attention to an uncomfortable situation.

At last! Dessert is served—a luscious piece of strawberry cheesecake. What a finale. Most likely a dessert fork or spoon will still be left at your place setting. If not, the waiter will serve one with the dessert. If one is not served and you can't find one, simply ask the waiter to bring you another.

The last thing you do when dinner is completely over is to blot your lips and place the napkin at the left side of your plate. This is an indicator to your waiter that you are finished and would like your bill.

Your bill will be on a piece of paper and will either be put on the table as is, presented on a small tray, or tucked in the inside cover of a small folder. Whatever form the bill is given to you is the same way you pay, but with the bill attached. The waiter will take it to the cashier and return your change.

Tips are traditionally figured to be 15 to 20 percent of your total bill before the tax. However, you may want to consider where you are, what you ordered, and the service given you.

If the service was excellent but the food mediocre, understand that the waiter has no control over the chef, and tip accordingly.

When the meal is over, it is permissible for the young lady to touch up her lipstick at the table if she does so discreetly. (A good time to do this is while the young man takes care of the bill.) A simple tube of lipstick and a small mirror should do.

Never touch or style your hair at the table. This is considered poor manners and can cause hair to fall on the table or in the food.

Now it's time to go. The young man should rise first and then assist the young lady with her chair.

What a meal! Not only did it taste good but you thoroughly enjoyed the company of your dinner companion because you were relaxed and knew just what to do.

Dining Do's and Don'ts

A young man who is wearing a heavy winter topcoat should hang it up or check it in when entering a nice restaurant. The young lady has the prerogative of either checking hers as well or wearing it directly to the table.

The cost of the coat and whether or not it matches her outfit should be considered in making the choice.

If you must sneeze during dinner, chances are you won't have time to locate a tissue or handkerchief. Grab your dinner napkin as you turn your head to the side, and sneeze as quietly as you can. Place your napkin back on your lap, and as you arrange it say quietly, "Excuse me, please." Don't look at anyone and say you are sorry or try to explain that you feel like you are getting sick. Drawing attention to the problem only makes it worse.

What if you had hot French onion soup and your nose is beginning to run? If you have a tissue, use it. If you don't, a last resort would be to use the edge of your napkin. Bring the napkin up to your mouth as though to blot your lips, and, while doing so, brush it by your nose. If, however, you are experiencing a major unleashing of the sinus passages, excuse yourself from the table and blow your nose in the restroom. Never honk at the table! It will gross everyone out.

If you must leave the table during dinner, do so without an explanation. If you announce why you are going you may upset your companions or embarrass yourself. Just leave and return as quickly as possible.

When you pass a pitcher of water or punch, turn the handle toward the other person. This makes it easy for them to reach out and take the handle.

It is not proper to eat directly from the serving dish. Take what you want from the tray and place it onto one of your dishes. Eat from your own dish.

Tasting another's food is all right if you pass your fork and have her put the morsel of food on your fork. Never reach over with your own silver and eat from her plate.

When eating at someone's home and seconds are offered, accept them if you wish. This is a compliment that shows you really enjoyed the food. Never ask for seconds. Your hostess may have only prepared enough for each person to have one serving and will be embarrassed.

54

Bacon may be eaten with either fork or fingers. The decision is based on how the bacon is cooked. Try your fork first. If the bacon is crispy and begins to shatter, you may pick it up with your fingers.

Do not put catsup, mustard, or condiments directly onto your food. Condiments should be placed to the side of your plate and applied to your food from there.

Butter and season an ear of corn one section at a time. If you butter the entire ear, the butter will drip off as you eat.

Don't eat corn on the cob in public unless you have a good supply of toothpicks. It tends to cling to and wedge between your teeth and can be very embarrassing.

The method of eating spaghetti by winding it on a fork held against a spoon is correct. When eating at a true Italian restaurant it is considered the only way to eat pasta. If you are at any other restaurant you may use your knife and fork and crosscut a small section of your pasta. Eat the section and then repeat. Don't massacre the entire plate of pasta at one time!

When dining out, a lady may place her purse on the floor, behind her on the chair, or in her lap. The place depends on the size of the purse and whether or not it has a shoulder strap.

As you eat clams or boiled shrimp, put the empty shells on the bowl or plate provided for you. If one is not provided, use your bread-and-butter plate.

Finger bowls that may have been placed on your table may contain warm water, a wedge of lemon, and have a napkin on top. When you are through with your shells, dip your fingers into the bowl and run the wedge of lemon across your fingers. This will cut the fishy smell and make your fingers smell and feel fresh.

If a restaurant provides you with eating utensils, you should use them. I know that french fries seem to taste better when you dip them into the catsup with your fingers, but if you have a fork, use it. Only at fast food restaurants should you use your fingers.

Pizza is considered a finger food. However, if you pick up the pizza and the end hangs down or the toppings start to slide off, put it back down and use a fork. When the crust is hard you may pick it back up.

Chicken or other fowl is to be deboned at the dinner table. Don't pick up a piece of chicken with your fingers unless you are at a picnic, at the Colonel's, or eating a tiny Cornish game hen.

As you bring food to your mouth, draw the food off of the utensil with your lips and not with your teeth.

When eating meals with gravy, it is permissible to "sop" the gravy with your bread. This is done with a fork, however, not your fingers.

Well, there you have it—all the basics that you will most likely need to dine with style. Study and practice them at home so they will become second nature to you when you eat out. Not only will you impress others with these skills but they will probably look to you as an example.

CHAPTER FIVE

DANCE
ETIQUETTE

For many teenagers, nothing is more fun than going to a dance. It's a great place to meet friends, relax, and cut loose. It's also a terrific way to meet new people. There are several rules of dance etiquette that will make your dances even more fun and rewarding.

A dance is probably the only event you will ever go to where it is considered all right to be fashionably late. This is how you make your grand entrance. You don't want to be more than thirty to forty-five minutes late, however, because you want to get in all the dances possible.

Be careful about selecting what you will wear to the dance. Dark colors tend to blend into the dark, and now is not the time to blend in. Wear either colors or a pattern that will stand out a little. Girls, you will never get asked to dance if no one knows you are there!

When you go to a dance, you may go with a large group of friends. Don't, however, stay in that large group once you are there. Break up into twos or threes. Guys find it embarrassing to approach a large herd of girls. They don't want to hurt anyone's feelings by asking only one girl to dance and ignoring all the others. Small groups are much more approachable.

After you and your friend separate from the group, you will want to make your rounds about the dance floor to see who's there and who you would really like to dance with.

Do this by slowly and nonchalantly walking around the entire circumference of the room. As you walk, chat briefly with your friend and look around. Once you have completed the circle and checked out all the prospects, you are now ready for the next step.

Girls, carefully select your target (otherwise known as dream man!). You now need to get within firing range. Position yourself about fifteen or twenty feet from him. Visit with your friend as you constantly look his way. Keep sweeping your eyes his way until he finally looks at you. The minute your eyes make contact, grin like a turkey, blush like crazy, and look at your friend with an "I can't believe I got caught" look.

By this time the guy is talking to his friend and telling him to look at the two cute girls to his left who have been staring at them. He will know for sure that you want to dance with him because your smile said it all.

The number one reason guys don't ask girls to dance is that they aren't sure the girls want to dance with them. Girls need to let the guys know that they are interested. Remember, when in doubt, he usually won't ask.

What about girls asking boys to dance? The best answer is, just *don't*—unless, of course, it's a girls' choice. If you do what I described, the guys will get the message. You'll find that you will be so busy dancing you won't have the time or the desire to ask them.

When a young man gets up enough courage to ask a girl to dance, she should always say yes. Never turn him down. There simply is no good reason why you can't dance just one dance with him. If you don't want to dance

58

with him again, that is your prerogative. You should, however, dance with him once.

After the young lady has accepted, the young man should take her hand and gently lead her onto the dance floor. If the dance is formal, he should place her hand gently over his forearm.

If the dance is a fast dance, the two of you will face each other and move to the music in whatever fashion strikes your fancy. If the dance is a slow dance, you will want to take dance position.

Contrary to what many may think, the bear hug is not considered dance position. (If you aren't familiar with this term, it's when the girl puts her arms around the neck of the guy and he puts his arms around her waist, and they stick together.) There are several reasons why you don't want to dance in this position. First, if you slow dance right after a fast dance, you may actually drip perspiration on each other. Not cool! Next, there is virtually no way you can carry on a conversation with this person when you are looking behind his or her back. It's like talking to a wall. Last of all is a biological reason: When you are that close to the opposite sex, your hormones go wild. If you really like the person, it's even worse. This is a normal and natural thing to happen. It's called being sexually attracted.

Danger! When these feelings take over, all your rational thinking takes a hike. It's easy to let your hormones overrule your good logic, and often these feelings and attractions are misinterpreted for feelings of love. Don't be deceived!

The purpose of a slow dance is to be in a close conversation position while moving to the music. It's delightful to look into your partner's eyes as you talk, to see his or her facial expressions, and to feel the warmth of the soul.

So how do you take dance position?

The young man should slip his left hand under the palm of the girl's right hand. Your palms will be touching,

and the girl's fingers will rest between the guy's thumb and index finger. Now the guy will bring his left arm up almost into a square position. (See illustration.) Next, he will rest his right hand on the girl's back slightly under her shoulder blade. As he does this, the girl will rest her left arm on top of his right arm with her fingertips touching the top seam of his shirtsleeve.

Once you have taken dance position it doesn't really matter what you do with your feet. If you happen to know some dance steps, use them. If you don't, just walk around the room to the beat of the music. You will have everyone thinking you are a wonderful dancer, when all you really know is a good dance position!

After the music ends, the young man should walk the young lady back to the place where he asked her to dance. He should thank her graciously, perhaps chat briefly, and then leave. This will keep the girl's interest, and she will want to dance with him again. If the guy just stands there forever, the challenge is gone and boredom may set in.

Dances that are the most fun are those in which everyone participates. Don't dance with just one person the entire evening. You will miss out on meeting lots of new people. Guys who are really classy will also make sure they ask several girls to dance who have not had the opportunity. Nothing will make you more popular than to have lots of girls think you are wonderful.

The only thing that could possibly make a dance more fun is to actually know some dance steps. If you have the opportunity to take a few dance classes and learn the basics, make sure you do so. You will find a whole new world of fun opened to you.

CHAPTER SIX

PROM
ETIQUETTE

Prom. The mere mention of the word brings visions of grandeur and conflict . . . young ladies in elegant dresses made of satin, velvet, and lamé . . . young men in tailored tuxedos with colorful cummerbunds . . . beautiful flowers with sweet, soft fragrances . . . delicious food at fancy restaurants . . . great music at a super dance . . . and, of course, prom pictures to remember the whole event.

Conflict! *What will I wear? Who will I ask? What if I don't get asked? How do you pin on corsages and boutonnieres? Will I know how to eat the right way? Can I dance with anyone besides my date? How do you act formally?*

Going to the prom isn't nearly so scary if you have some basic guidelines. This chapter will cover ways to make your prom date not only comfortable but maybe even the best date of the year!

The first prom question is *Who will I ask?* or *What if I don't get asked?* This is less of a problem for the guys because prom is considered a boy-ask-girl event. Since the guys do the asking, they simply need to make up their minds who the lucky girls will be. Guys might want to take into consideration that this will probably be their most expensive date of the year. Because you will be spending so much money, you will want to choose a date you know you'll have fun with. If you ask a girl you don't know very well or have never been out with, you're running a big risk.

Make a list of three young women you would really enjoy taking. Choose your favorite of the three, and ask her first. You may think this is silly, but if the one you ask already has a date, you have two other options. It can be devastating if you have only one choice and she can't go.

Because this is such a special date, you will want to do a few things differently.

First, ask your date to the prom at least one week in advance, preferably two. Try not to ask more than two weeks ahead. If you ask too far in advance, it can take away some of the excitement.

Next, ask your date in a creative way. A phone call isn't very creative. Use your imagination. Think of something fun and out of the ordinary.

Don't make it too difficult! A young lady extended an invitation to my son, Talmadge, by putting her question on different strips of shredded paper. The idea was good, but she put the question strips into a garbage bag full of shredded paper. He spent more than an hour looking before he asked me for help. We then spent more than two hours looking through shredded paper trying to find the strips to complete the message. After two hours of tedious searching, hands that were filthy from print copy, and a room that was completely trashed with fifteen million pieces of paper, we gave up.

The next day at school, my son had to have an announcement made over the intercom, asking the young lady who extended the invitation (whoever she was) to please contact him. She was embarrassed, and so was he.

If you need a few suggestions on ways to ask someone out, ask your friends what they have done. Some additional ideas may be found in the chapter "Creative Dating Ideas."

It's always polite to answer an invitation within a day or two. Don't take a week to respond just so you can see if someone else will ask. Your decision should be based on whether you want to go with that person, not *Who are my choices?*

If you cannot go, answer as soon as possible so he can find another date. Don't leave him hanging!

When you are asked out in a creative way, you might give your answer in the same manner. It will then be as much fun for him to receive the answer as it was to ask.

Oh no! No one asked you to prom. Oh well, we can just stay at home and later enjoy listening to everyone else tell us about their good time, right?

Wrong! You only have two proms in your entire life, a junior prom and a senior prom. Don't miss either one.

Young ladies who haven't been asked have two options. First, you can ask someone from a different school. This is quite appropriate, especially if you have already gone out with him.

The second choice is to find out which of the guys at your school are not going to prom. The number one reason that a guy doesn't go is money. Ask a guy who is a good friend of yours, but not a dating friend.

You might say, "Sam, are you taking Jenny to prom? Oh, that's too bad she already had another date. I was hoping Bob would ask me, but he asked someone else. Hey, since neither one of us has dates, why don't we get a few friends together and all go stag? That way we can all go and have fun, and it won't cost any of us a ton of money!"

Most guys who don't have a date would jump at the chance to go with a friend on a group date instead of missing prom. Because it's more of a group thing than a date, you can feel comfortable about splitting the cost of everything. Each person pays for his own ticket, dinner, and pictures.

In this case, flowers are not necessary. However, you might want to consider giving flowers or a boutonniere to your friend with the understanding that the flowers are a "thank you." Attach a note with a short message on it to make sure this is clear.

Otherwise, flowers are always appropriate on prom dates. The young man should ask the girl what color her dress is at least three days before the date. He can then order flowers that coordinate. If you want to surprise the girl, however, call her mother and ask. The mother will be impressed not only that you were brave enough to call and talk to her but also that you care enough about detail to coordinate everything.

Girls should check with their dates to find out the color of their tuxes and cummerbunds. (Guys like things to match too!) Try to match the color of the boutonniere with the cummerbund. If you can't match exactly, choose red. It's a classic and will go with anything.

Young men should always check ahead of time to make reservations for dinner. If you haven't eaten at that restaurant before, you may want to find out what kinds of food are served and the price range.

It's also a good idea to order your tuxedo at least one week in advance. A lot of different school proms are held on the same night. If you wait until the last minute, you may not get the selection or size you want.

Always bring more money than you think the date will cost. You never know when prices will change, and you certainly don't want to be caught short on such an important night.

At last! You have a prom date. Dinner reservations are made. Flowers are ordered. You are ready.

Guys, the morning of your prom date, pick up the flowers and your tuxedo. Make a quick call to the restaurant to reconfirm your dinner reservations. Now take a nap and relax. You deserve it. You're one efficient guy!

Young ladies should make sure they plan everything ahead as well. Don't leave the decision of what you are going to wear until the last minute. If you go shopping a day or two before the prom, you can bet that the dresses will all be picked over.

Formal does not mean your dress has to be brief. Many a young man has been surprised and sometimes disappointed at the lack of material on a formal dress. Use the same standards of good grooming and dressing for prom as you would for other events.

If you decided to wear your hair up or in a different style than usual, do a dry run a day or two before prom. Many tears have been shed by young ladies who try a new look for prom and the new look looks terrible.

Boutonnieres should be ordered several days ahead and picked up the morning of the prom date.

Finally, that special day is here! Pick up your boutonniere that morning and then relax for a couple of hours before you get ready. Sleep will probably be impossible because of your excitement. That's OK, just rest.

Make sure you give yourself plenty of time to get ready for your big date. When you're rushed you have a tendency to get nervous and uptight. This feeling will carry over into the evening.

Now, relax and get ready to enjoy a wonderful evening. After all, you deserve it. You are completely prepared.

It's time! Your date said he would pick you up at six o'clock. As always, you were ready ten minutes early because you know a lady never keeps her gentleman friend waiting. When your date knocks at the door, make sure you are there to answer. It is so much fun to open the door and see the look on his face when he sees that not only are you ready but you look radiant!

Invite your date in for a minute so you can introduce him to your parents, if they don't already know him, and exchange flowers. Make sure you tell your date how great he or she looks. Girls have spent hours getting ready and are thrilled when their dates tell them how gorgeous they look. Remember that guys also have taken

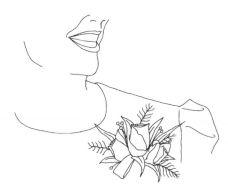

a long time to prepare for this date, and they will love to be told how handsome they look as well.

If this is a group date, or if the girl extended the invitation, the young man should offer to pick up the girl. If he doesn't offer, the young lady should make the suggestion.

Most corsages for young girls have both a pin and an elastic band attached. This way she has the choice of how to wear the flower. If she chooses to wear it on her wrist, the young man can hold it as she slips her left hand through the elastic. If she decides to wear it attached to her dress, I would recommend she ask her mother for assistance. Pinning corsages on dresses can be quite cumbersome.

The correct way to attach the flower is to insert a pin into the fabric and back up first to pick up a small piece of the material. Now insert the pin into the lower part of the corsage stem where the main bulk of the flower is being supported. Once through the stem continue the pin back down into the fabric again. If the dress is lined with a second layer of material, insert the pin between the two layers and leave it there. When there is no second layer, bring the pin back up and leave it slightly exposed. Never leave the pin point down through the dress. It may eventually give your date a terrible stab. Repeat the process with a second pin at the top of the corsage. This will ensure that the flower will be securely attached.

Boutonnieres are pinned on in the exact same manner as the corsage except in a different location and with only one pin. They may also be pinned starting from underneath the lapel so the head of the pin doesn't show. Corsages are placed on the upper left shoulder of the young lady but not so the flower extends too much above her shoulder bone. The boutonniere is attached to the left lapel of the young man's tuxedo toward the top, but not covering the buttonhole. (See illustration.)

Young ladies should always pin the flower on the young man. It is very difficult for him to perform this feat looking upside down.

Flowers are attached, compliments exchanged, and curfews confirmed. (Though you don't usually confirm curfews at the door, you may want to for this date. Prom dates are usually quite lengthy, and you will want to make sure that you have enough time for everything.) Now you're off!

Because this is a formal date, you will definitely want to escort your date to the car in the manner discussed in the dating chapter. (Remember, fingertips over forearm!) The young man may even need to assist the young lady in making sure that her long dress is all in the car. (I once saw a young couple going to prom with the young lady's dress hanging out of the car and dragging on the wet pavement. Can you imagine the look on the poor girl's face when she got out of the car and saw her dress muddy and possibly torn!)

Your first stop will probably be at a nice restaurant or at someone's home. My sons often choose to have the formal dinner at our home in order to save both time and money. If you choose this, please make sure that your home is completely void of all your brothers and sisters—unless, of course, you have persuaded or paid them to serve and clean up. Also, make sure the meal is planned and cooked in advance. You will definitely want to consult your mother on this. She will be happy to help you have a wonderful dinner and save money too.

Turn to the chapter on dining etiquette and review all the "right" things to do before you go out to eat. If you have already been practicing them at your family dinner table, not only will your mother be in total ecstasy but you will also feel very comfortable.

After a lovely dinner, you are now ready for the big dance.

When you arrive at the dance, have your pictures taken first. This will ensure that the young lady will appear fresh and not have that wilted look that so often occurs after several fast dances.

Believe it or not, there is a proper way to stand when having prom pictures taken. I have seen so many pictures of prom couples that are disastrous because feet were wide apart or the girl was not sure what to do with her arm. She hooked it over the guy's arm and left it dangling in midair in the center of the picture like a limp fish.

From now on this will never happen to you. When friends look at your prom pictures they will wonder why you looked so poised and professional and they don't.

Gentlemen, your position is easy. Stand facing the camera with your head high, back straight, and feet four to six inches apart. Your left arm will be brought up, palm toward your abdomen, fingers relaxed, and just below your belt buckle. Drop your right arm to the side.

Young ladies, since you are standing to the left of your date, you should take your left foot and point it straight toward the camera in a twelve o'clock position. The right foot should be placed behind the left foot and turned out in a two o'clock position. The left heel will be touching the arch or center of the right foot.

As you take this foot position, your body will be turned slightly toward the young man. Now take your right hand and place the fingertips through his arm and over the middle of his forearm. (This is the same position you take when you are being escorted to the car.) Your left arm will drop to your left side, or, if you really like him, you can place your left hand over his left arm also.

In this case, if the fellow really likes you he may choose to put his right hand over your left hand.

Just wait till you get your pictures back. You will absolutely love them!

At last, the dance. Cut loose, have fun, but don't forget to take dance position for your slow dances. (Refer to the dance chapter for this position.) You will look like Cinderella and Prince Charming to all those who are watching.

Can you trade dances with other couples even though you came as a date or a group?

By all means. It's always fun to mingle with others. But don't just leave your date or group and go your merry way. Make sure your date has someone else to dance with or at least visit with while you are gone. Also, if you choose to dance with others, dance with your own date in between each dance. Never make your date feel neglected. If you sense your date feels uncomfortable about the changing of partners, discontinue it or else hold it to a minimum.

What a fun time!

If you have planned an activity after the dance, you need to take your date home for a quick change of clothes, unless you have made other arrangements ahead of time.

When the date is completely over, it's time to go home.

You may want to turn to the dating chapter to refresh your memory on how to end the date. I will add, however, that a quick kiss on the cheek would be most appropriate to end such a special date.

Thank you's are always appropriate. Since this was such an expensive date for both parties, a thank you is in order for each.

Young men, a thank-you note with a single rose attached will make her remember you forever. She will tell every girl in school what a fantastic date you are.

Young ladies, a note sent with a plate of cookies or candy will make him think you are the "sweetest" date he ever had. He will tell all his friends how thoughtful you are.

There you have it—guidelines that will help your prom date be not only fun but one of your most memorable dates in high school.

CHAPTER SEVEN

PUBLIC ETIQUETTE

Church and Theater

You have probably never thought about any rules or guidelines for church, live theater, or movies. There are several, however, that should be observed so all who attend may enjoy the event.

The appropriate dress for church and live theater is a dress or skirt for young ladies and dress slacks and ties for young men. At church this shows reverence for sacred things, while at the theater it shows respect for those performing.

Think about others as you arrive and walk into the building. If someone ahead of you reaches out to hold the door open, make sure you thank him or her and place your hand on the door to hold it for the next person. Many times I have seen some polite soul hold the door open while a herd of people push through—ignoring any obligation to help anyone else!

Always ar-
rive at least ten
minutes early.
This will allow
you time to
choose a good
seat or have the
usher assist you.
You will also be
able to look
through the pro-
gram and know
how the event
will proceed.

If, for some unspeakable reason, you are late for church, be as inconspicuous as you can. Sit in the back if possible. Never walk in late and proceed to the first couple of rows. This is not the time for a grand entry. It disrupts the entire meeting.

Being late for the theater where a live performance is taking place is inexcusable. The doors are usually closed at starting time and aren't opened again until intermission. No matter how good your excuse is for being late, you will miss the entire first act.

Occasionally ushers will show you to your seat. The lady should follow the usher, and the young man or date should follow the lady. When you go to the theater as a couple, the young man has the prerogative to choose the row, and the young lady chooses the seat.

As you pass others in the row to take your seat, if you know the people, face them with your back to the stage or podium. If you don't know them, face the stage with your back to them. In either case say, "Excuse me, please," or, if they happen to rise, say, "Thank you."

In a church meeting where hymns are being sung, be aware of those around you who might need a book. If you have extras, share with them.

Do not play with the program or tear it into pieces.

Not only does this cause noise, but when you leave it looks like a troupe of little mice has marched through.

Keep whispering to a bare minimum. Whispering annoys those around you and makes the speaker or performer wonder if she has done something objectionable of if you are talking about her.

Pay close attention to the speaker or performer by looking at her. This tells her that her message is being received. If possible, have a pleasant expression on your face. I have spoken to groups where everyone had a scowl or blank expression. It really makes you feel uncomfortable.

When the meeting or performance is over, feel free to go up and express your feelings or compliment the performer or speaker. You may think this would bother the performer or speaker, but it doesn't. Anytime someone takes the time to pay a compliment, it is always greatly appreciated.

Never play "beauty shop" in a public place. Braiding hair and fixing makeup or nails is considered personal grooming and should be done in private. Doing this in public makes you look like the monkeys at the zoo who groom each other!

Be careful about displaying physical affection in public also. It is so embarrassing to sit behind a couple who are continually rubbing, stroking, or kissing each other.

After the meeting is over, exit on the side you entered. If you are there as a couple, the young woman should exit on the young man's side and allow him to wait and hold the row open for her. This way you won't get lost from each other in the crowd.

Other Situations

Manners apply everywhere, especially in public. Courtesies shown in public make being around large groups of people much more comfortable.

When you walk down a sidewalk or in the mall, always keep to the right. This allows a smooth flow of traffic.

Gentlemen should always walk on the outside or closest to the street when walking with a lady. This protects her from being pushed off or having anything splashed on her.

A lady accompanied by two gentlemen should always walk in the center. This works in reverse if there are two ladies and one gentleman. The purpose for this positioning is to ensure that everyone will be included in the conversation. When two people of the same sex get together, they tend to leave out the other person.

In public as in the home, a lady precedes a gentleman going up or down stairs. If the stairs are slippery, however, the gentleman may choose to go down first in order to catch the young lady if she slips.

Women always go first through revolving doors. This way if she can't get out, the man will be there to rescue her!

Avoid loud talking, pushing, or walking with arms linked around each other's waist. Not only does this draw attention to you, but no one enjoys walking behind a couple who is constantly bumping bottoms as they walk.

It is permissible now for a young lady to use a powder puff or lipstick in public if she can manage it discreetly. However, she should never use a comb or brush, and by all means she shouldn't adjust any lingerie straps in public.

A lady precedes a man when boarding a bus, but the man precedes the lady when leaving. He can then be of assistance if she needs help (or catch her if she falls!).

A young man should never sit in his car to carry on a conversation with a young lady standing on the sidewalk. This gives the appearance that he is trying to "pick her up." If you wish to visit with her, make sure you get out of your car to talk. This shows you respect her.

Never sit in your car and honk the horn for someone to come out. Always get out and ring the doorbell or else have the person wait at the door and watch for you until you arrive.

Gentlemen should step aside for a lady to get on and off an elevator first. He should hold the elevator doors if they begin to close.

Men should always remove their hats when entering a building, when a prayer is being said, or when the national anthem and Pledge of Allegiance are being presented. Women may wear their hats in a building and are not required to remove them for any reason.

When yawning, always cover your mouth with your hand and say, "Excuse me." No one enjoys seeing your dental work!

Rules, rules, rules. Did you ever think you would read so many at one time? Are they really necessary?

Absolutely! Because we live in such a busy and crowded world, public manners are more important than ever. When common courtesies are extended to others, life seems to flow more smoothly and be more orderly.

Remember, the Golden Rule—"Do unto others as you would have them do unto you"—is not dead, it's just rusty.

CHAPTER EIGHT

FAMILY ETIQUETTE

With all the information and ideas available on how to make people feel comfortable, why do we tend to drop them all as we walk through the front door of our home? Suddenly the rule "anything goes" comes into effect. If we should be considerate of anyone it should be our family members—after all, we live with them on a daily basis. (Besides, they see us at our very worst and could blackmail us to our adoring public at any time.)

This chapter is devoted to teaching courtesies that will make our home life run smoother while making our family members think we are totally awesome. (They might even want to go out of their way to do something special for us!)

The best way to do this is to go through a day with the family from start to finish.

In preparing for this chapter I asked several families I know well to sit down and think of some suggestions for things that they either do in their own families or would like to see done. I was amazed at the similarities between families. Apparently a lot of families have the same complaints and woes. You will probably want to share what you learn from this chapter with the rest of your family.

"Good morning!" "Morning." "Ugh!" All three greetings are indicative of our attitudes toward morning. For some it is good, for others it is OK, and for a few it is ugly!

I found a nightshirt at an airport gift store that best describes how I feel about mornings. It has a picture of a bunny rabbit in PJ's and large house slippers. One ear is bent over and hair curlers are falling off its head as it takes a sip of hot chocolate. The caption reads, "I don't DO mornings!" I bought it!

For some of us, mornings are the hardest part of the day. It takes at least an hour of moving around or a ten-minute hot shower to wake us up. Please be considerate of us. Either don't speak to us or point us to the shower. We will be fine as soon as we are completely awake.

For those of you who turn off the alarm and hop out of the bed bright and cheery, ready to start a new day— we hate you! Not really. The truth is, we admire you and would love to be that way, but our bodies just don't function the same.

The first step of the day is to wake up. If you have your own room, you can hit the snooze alarm as many times as you choose. If you share a room, however, force yourself out of bed. Don't disturb the sleep of your roommate.

Once you are up, don't turn on the overhead light. To a sleeping person, a sudden light is not only rude but startling. He may knock something over as he reaches to throw any available object at you. Instead, turn on a soft lamp or a small light from your closet.

Next, it's off to the shower. Unless you have your own bathroom (and a mother who never looks in it), you will want to remember several things that are annoying to others.

78

Don't drop your dirty underwear in the middle of the floor and leave it there. Most smart moms have a clothes receptical that you can place soiled clothing in.

While in the shower, if you use the last of the shampoo, rinse, or bath soap, take the bottles out and either replace them or at least inform the next person that they are empty. Few things are more frustrating than to discover that you will have to get out of the shower dripping wet to find some replacements.

Before you leave the shower, check to see if there are any hair balls around, and remove them. That is a sure gross-out for the next person.

Dry yourself off before you get out of the shower, or step on a bath mat or hand towel. No one likes to walk or slide on a wet floor or to get their socks soggy.

Be aware of how much hot water is available in your home, and make sure you save some for the next person. Also know how many others need the bathroom, and don't spend too much time in the shower.

Don't leave your towel wadded up on the floor to sour and mildew. Hang it up, or, if your mom prefers, put it in the dirty-clothes basket.

Now reach into the shower and take your washcloth, wring it out, and treat it the same way you did your towel. Don't leave a soggy washcloth in the shower for others to squish on.

Ah! What a wonderful shower. You are nice and awake now. Time to brush your teeth.

After you squeeze the toothpaste, put the lid back on and put it away. Don't leave it out with the cap off to drip all over the counter or crust over.

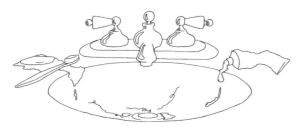

Try your best not to splatter anything onto the bathroom mirror. If you do, wipe it off with a towel.

When you rinse out your mouth, don't forget to rinse out the sink as well. The ultimate gross-out is to look down at the sink and see someone else's salivary remains.

If you need to use the bathroom for "personal" reasons, please be considerate of the next person. Don't use the last square of toilet paper without replacing it with a new roll. (I had to have a special meeting with my family to demonstrate how to replace the roll. Seems no one knew!)

Always place the toilet seat back down. Make sure you leave the bathroom clean and pleasant for the next person.

The last rule on the bathroom is, if you brought it in, you take it out. This keeps things from getting cluttered.

We are now out of the bathroom and off to our room to get dressed. Modesty is appreciated at any age, so make sure your body is covered adequately with a large towel or bathrobe as you travel from one room to the next.

Selecting what you are going to wear for the day isn't too hard for guys. You just grab the nearest pair of Levi's that are semi-clean and any shirt within reach. (After all, nothing clashes with denim.) For girls, however, it's a little more complicated. Skirt or pants? Dressy or casual? And of course, everything must color-coordinate!

If you pull several outfits out of your closet to consider, make sure you hang up the ones you don't wear. A good rule of thumb in helping to keep your room picked up is "If it's clean, hang it up. If it's dirty, put it in the dirty-clothes basket."

Before you leave your room, make sure your bed is made. Mothers feel they are successful if their children's rooms are straightened up and their beds are made. It not only puts them in a good mood but also gives you bargaining power if you need to ask Mom for a favor. How can she refuse a child who is so neat and organized?

Now it's off to the kitchen for a good breakfast.

If you are fortunate enough to have a mother who cooks you a hot breakfast, make sure you thank her for her efforts. Remember, she could have slept in and left you to get a bowl of cold cereal. Do this by clearing your dishes from the table, putting them into the dishwasher or sink, and giving her a quick kiss on the cheek as you leave, saying, "Thanks, Mom."

That's it! Your mother will now think she has the most thoughtful and considerate child in the world and will do almost anything for you. (It's amazing how far being nice to parents will get you!)

As you leave for school, make sure your parents are aware of any plans you may have for the afternoon or evening. This helps the family to coordinate schedules with cars, rides, and such and makes things run more smoothly on the home front.

What a day! School is over, and you are back home.

When you walk through the front door, don't drop your books and coat in the entry area. This is the first place guests see, and Mom wants it to always look tidy. Unload in the kitchen or in your room (which is the final book destination, anyway!).

Because it's been three or more hours since you had lunch, most moms don't mind your having an afternoon snack. It's harder to study when your blood sugar is low. Besides, you need a break.

The kitchen is probably the most used and most popular room in the house. It seems as though everything revolves around food! There are several things to remember that will help make the kitchen scene more pleasant for all.

Nothing is more refreshing than a nice cold glass of milk to drink with your snack. Make sure, however, that you put the carton back into the fridge. Milk that has become warm from sitting out on the counter is a real gross-out.

If you take the last cookie out of the bag, don't put

the bag back on the shelf. It is really disappointing to see a bag of delicious cookies, get all geared up to chow down on some, and then discover that the bag is empty. The same thing pertains to finding an empty juice pitcher in the fridge. It's really frustrating!

When you use the last ice cube, remember to refill the ice trays for others. After all, someone else did that for you, or you wouldn't be enjoying your ice.

After you have finished your snack, place your dirty dishes in the sink or dishwasher and wipe any crumbs off the table. Your mom will wonder who the mystery snacker was who left no trail of crumbs behind!

Do your homework now without being told—such is the dream of every parent. Parents just love studious children. Besides, your chances of doing an evening activity improve tremendously if your homework is out of the way.

If both your parents work, don't dump all your troubles on them when they walk through the front door. Their blood sugar is low too, and they have just battled the five o'clock traffic. Whatever you tell them that is unpleasant will seem magnified tenfold. Help them to throw dinner on and then hit them with the bad stuff after they are fed and relaxed. Chances are the problems will seem more manageable and stay in proportion.

One of the best things for a family to do to stay close is to eat the evening meal together. I know this is a real feat nowadays. Juggling everyone's schedule to accommodate this will be challenging, but it's worth the trouble. If your family doesn't do this already, you might recommend it.

Eating together can be pleasant if you remember a few basic courtesies.

Wait to begin eating or serving until everyone has been seated and a blessing has been offered. No one likes someone who thinks of himself first and does a total pig-out for all to see.

Serve yourself from the dish closest to you, and then

pass it to the next person. Keep in mind that others are eating as well. Remember to leave them an adequate or equal amount. For a detailed account of dining manners, turn to the chapter on dining. Home is the best place to practice these manners. Not only will you make your parents happy that they have such well-mannered children but you will become comfortable with these practices. They will become second nature for you as you eat with people you really want to impress.

"Please" and "thank you" are always appropriate and appreciated phrases when speaking to anyone, especially your family. Use them generously when asking for or receiving something.

During dinner, keep your conversation positive. Now is not the time to tell your family about the gory accident you heard about at school or that you may be failing math. These unpleasantries can bring about arguments and can totally disrupt the digestion process.

After dinner, don't play the disappearing game unless Mom gets to play too. Moms get very unhappy and grouchy when they have been left behind to face a sinking ship of dirty dishes.Place your dishes in the sink or dishwasher. Now go back to the table and remove several items that need to be put away. With each family member doing his or her part, kitchen clean-up becomes a snap.

Evening seems to be the time when every family member either needs to use the telephone or is expecting an "important" phone call. For this reason, phone courtesies are especially important.

Keep calls brief. Five to ten minutes should be enough to convey important messages. If more time is needed, arrange to see the other party in person.

If someone is on the phone and you need to make a call, don't keep picking up the receiver to see if she is finished. This is extremely rude. It makes her think you are eavesdropping on her conversation. Go into the room she is in to see if she's finished. Should she be over her allotted time, don't yell into the room with the announcement. Simply go in and pretend to hold a phone up to your ear and then point to your watch. This is a direct hint that her time is up and you need the phone.

Be careful to keep background noise to a minimum. It's hard to listen to someone on the other end of the phone when the TV is turned up or a loud conversation is in progress.

Don't tell a family member that someone called but didn't leave a name. They will sweat bullets trying to figure out who called. If the caller didn't leave a name or a message, the call was probably unimportant and doesn't need to be reported.

When taking messages for someone, make sure you write down the date, time, name, and number of the caller. Good phone messages are appreciated by all family members. If you take good messages for them, they will take good messages for you. (For more details on phone manners, turn to the chapter on phone skills.)

There are several other courtesies that help family life run smoother. As you read these, see if any of them sound familiar.

Don't borrow anything, especially clothing, without permission from the owner. Nothing fires up a family feud faster than to see the shirt you planned to wear that day walk out the front door on your brother or sister. When you do have permission, make sure you return the shirt or object in clean or useable condition.

Throw away yucky tissues instead of leaving them lying around to infect others.

Television during school nights should be kept to a minimum. The sound of a TV blaring throughout the house is not conducive to studying. Most teens who make good grades and participate in athletic or musical activities don't have much time to watch—they have other things to spend their valuable time on. If you find that you are spending a lot of time in front of the set, find a hobby that interests you or maybe a sport or musical activity of some kind. Most parents are more than happy to assist you when finances are available.

Occasionally we all feel down. Don't go around the house, however, with an angry or depressed look on your face. This brings others down as well. If you have a problem, discuss it with another family member. They are usually willing to help. Friends may come and go, but a family is always there to help and support you.

A little poem read by the Apostle LeGrand Richards gives the best advice ever for handling problems. The poem says:

> For every worry under the sun
> There is a remedy, or there is none.
> If there is a remedy, hurry and find it.
> If there is none, never mind it.

As you watch a video with the family, don't tell the ending or punch line if you have seen the film before. This blows the film for everyone else.

When someone calls out your name, respond immediately. Don't wait for your name to be repeated over and over. As beautiful as your name is, it is very annoying for others to keep hearing it, especially when they know you heard it the first time.

Always knock when the door to a room you want to enter is closed. Wait for a response to be invited in. If there is none, you may feel free to enter.

Friends who visit should obey all the rules of your home. It is your duty to fill them in. They should never wander through the private areas of your home. (Your parents' room is the biggest no-no of all!)

Many families enjoy teasing each other. Not only is it fun, it can also be a healthy means of communication. Teasing to the point of tears, however, is wrong. Never find your laughs at the expense of another's feelings. When hurt feelings are first detected, back off and apologize. We all have our sensitive spots. Be respectful of them.

As your day draws to an end, it's time to get ready for bed. Don't forget your bathroom courtesies as you wash your face and brush your teeth.

If you really want your mom to eat out of your hand, remember to do the following before you go to bed: Put your dirty clothes in their designated place. Kiss your mom on the cheek and tell her you love her. Be in bed on time. These acts will confirm to your mother that she has without a doubt the most thoughtful and considerate child in the world. She will now give you anything—not! But she would if she could!

The main thing to remember in dealing with your family is to treat them with all the kindness and respect that you would a guest—even when they don't deserve it. You will find that if you follow the simple suggestions listed in this chapter, your family will be much closer and home life will truly be "a little piece of heaven on earth."

Wow! Did you ever think there could be so many right things to do? Most rules of etiquette make good sense. They are simply ways to assist or make others feel comfortable. (Remember the number one rule of thumb on etiquette found in chapter 1!)

When you learn to treat others with respect and dignity, you will find that that is most often how they will treat you. Life will be a lot more fun and rewarding for you and for all those you meet. You will be making a great contribution to your community and to the individuals in it!

CHAPTER NINE

CREATIVE DATING IDEAS

Back in the "olden" days there were very few ways to ask someone out. You either asked her in person or you gave her a call on the phone and said, "Would you like to go out with me?" Real creative, right?

The dates were about as creative as the invitation. You either went to a movie, out to eat, or maybe to an athletic event. Boring—if that's all you ever did.

Dating in the nineties is totally different. Someone finally figured out that the purpose of dating is to get to know someone better. That's impossible when you are both staring at a movie screen.

The best dates are those that are so much fun you hate to see them end. It's as though you wished there would be a sequel—part two and part three. You laugh, you talk, you totally relax and enjoy yourself and the company you are with. Now, that's a great date!

This chapter contains tried and true ideas for unique dates, as well as ideas for creative ways to ask someone out. Read through them and find a few that fit your personality and circumstances; then call some friends, make some plans, and go for it. You'll be surprised how much more fun dating will be.

1. Have a Japanese dinner. Buy chopsticks and eat sitting on the floor.
2. Try a pots-and-pans dinner. Set a table with pans, spatulas, and so on, then put a sheet over it to hide the utensils. The couples won't know what is going on, so tell them to pick a seat. Serve spaghetti or something else that is difficult to eat. They must use the utensils they are given—for example, one person may have to eat with a spatula out of a frying pan. Serve drinks out of vases. It's embarrassing and fun!
3. Have a candlelight dinner on the steps of the state capitol building with waiters and violin music. Keep the whole thing secret beforehand.
4. Have a steak fry and play volleyball.
5. Have a catered candlelight dinner in the mountains.
6. Go to a park in a canyon and roast marshmallows and hot dogs. Sit around a campfire and sing songs and talk.
7. Have a square dance with everyone dressed up in old garb.
8. Go waterskiing with a group and have a cookout.
9. Go to a ballet, symphony, or visit an art gallery. Your date will be impressed with how classy you are!
10. Try a snow picnic. Come dressed like explorers of the Arctic wilderness in goggles, huge coats, and so on. Bring big rubber duck decoys and hike through the snow up a canyon. Build a fire and have a picnic.
11. Plan a day of horseback riding.

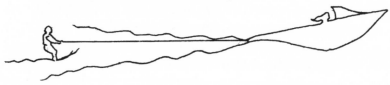

12. Get a bunch of old Little Rascals films or cartoons and show them. Afterward, make a Japanese dinner.
13. Go canoeing.
14. Go to the gym to swim and play paddleball.
15. Go sledding or tobagganing.
16. Have a waffle party. The hostess provides the waffle batter, drinks, and other necessities.
17. Try a "toe painting" party. Use finger paints with your toes! Serve homemade pizza and ice cream.
18. Go tubing on a river, followed by a barbecue.
19. Fix a gourmet dinner together with things you have never tasted or eaten before. Have each person bring his favorite story, poem, record, or piece of music and put on a presentation for the others, telling why it means something to him.
20. Get up early and go to breakfast (3:00 A.M.) at one of your houses or at an all-night restaurant.'
21. Have tinfoil dinners up in a canyon.
22. Test-drive a Jaguar or Porsche.
23. Have a kite-flying contest with several other couples. Give awards for the kite that soars the highest, crashes the most, and so on.
24. Tie-dye T-shirts.
25. Have water-gun wars.
26. Have a scavenger hunt called "Bigger or Better." Give each group a penny and have them go around a neighborhood trading it for something that is either better (worth more) or larger in size. Set a time limit and decide on a place to meet. The group with the biggest and best item wins.
27. Play Twister.
28. Go ice blocking.
29. Go to a rodeo.
30. Have a coupon date. Use coupons for different fast-food restaurants. At one place get a hamburger, at another get ice cream, at another get drinks, and so on.
31. Make your own home video with dates.

32. Have a picnic in a dome tent on top of a trampoline. Have the tent and trampoline decorated with streamers, confetti, balloons, and signs.

33. Play water balloon volleyball. Each couple takes one towel and holds it by the end corners. Using the towel, they both catch and throw the balloon across the net.

34. Go to a mall and have a scavenger hunt for names. For example, get the signatures of a person buying a hamburger, a student at the local college, a person with a shoe size bigger than 15, a person wearing a hat, and so on.

35. Have a pool party and watch *Jaws.*

36. Have a budget dinner. This date should be done in a group of at least six couples. Everyone goes to a grocery store and breaks up into teams, two couples in each team. The teams have about three to four dollars to buy either a main dish, dessert, or drink. Meet in three minutes, buy the food, and eat up.

37. Set a really nice table for dinner. After all the couples arrive, take off the tablecloth, spread aluminum foil on the table, and dump dinner in the middle. No silverware allowed.

38. Videotape your own commercials.

39. Play water baseball. Use children's swimming pools for bases and Slip-n-Slide for home plate.

40. Have a theme date where everything that happens on the date revolves around the theme. Possible themes: red, lemon, Japanese, and so on.

Some dates are still pretty standard. Prom, sweetheart ball, and homecoming are just a few. To spice up these dates, try using a creative way to extend your invitation. The following ideas may help jog your own creativity.

1. Write your invitation on the back of a puzzle and put the pieces in a small gift-wrapped box. Make sure you include a message on a small piece of paper ex-

plaining that in order to find out who wants to take him or her on the date, the puzzle will have to be put together.

2. Include your invitation in a homemade video. You can be the star who does the asking, or let your imagination go wild and use crazy friends or even a professional actor.

3. Throw pictures of big lips on the front lawn of your friend's house with a sign stuck in the ground that says, "I'd kiss the ground you walk on if you would go to _____ with me."

4. Put goldfish in their bathroom sink or tub. On a floating boat, attach a note that says, "Out of all the fish in the sea, you're the one I want to go to _____ with me." (Make sure you have permission from his or her parents.)

5. Place a message inside a decorated candy egg or a plastic egg that says, "I would be so egg-cited if you would go to _____ with me."

6. Give a tiny pair of boxing gloves and a rose with this poem attached:

> He floats like a butterfly,
> Stings like a bee—
> I'd be knocked out
> If you went to _____ with me.

7. Send your prospective date on a treasure hunt with clues scattered in a mall. At the end there will be a tiny treasure chest with gold candy coins and a note reading, "It would be my 'good fortune' if you would go to _____ with me."

8. Have the invitation announced at a school function or athletic event.

9. Buy a box of alphabet cereal and color letters for each word in your message. Include instructions on grouping each color for each word to find out who wants to take him or her to the event.

10. Freeze the message into a block of ice.
11. Take a roll of toilet paper and write a story on it. In the middle of the story write, "By the way, will you go to _____ with me?"
12. If you know a police officer, have him or her pull your friend over while driving or go to your friend's home and deliver the invitation verbally.
13. Give a photo frame with a message that says, "Picture this—I want to take you to _____." Include pictures of yourself and your prospective date.
14. Have a friend present a scroll with the words cut out from magazines instead of your handwriting.
15. Write a message on poster board, using candy bars to replace some of the words. Example: "Hey, 'Big Hunk' [the candy bar], you would be a 'Life Saver' [the candy roll] if you would go to _____ with me."
16. Mail a tape recording with the invitation on it.
17. Use an animal theme to deliver the message. Example: Attach a note to a small stuffed bear that says, "I couldn't 'bear' to go to _____ without you."
18. Fill an inexpensive wine glass with candy coins. Attach a note that says, "I would toast my good fortune if you would go to _____ with me."
19. Bake a cake and put the invitation between the icing layers.
20. Give a bag of fortune cookies with your name hidden in one. Include this note: "It would be my 'good fortune' if you would go to _____ with me."

I hope that these ideas have put your creative thought processes into action and that you are thinking of other great ideas. Just remember to keep it simple and make it fun. Not only will your dates love going out with you, they will have had a great time being asked.

ABOUT THE AUTHOR

A native of Atlanta, Georgia, Vivian R. Cline is a prominent speaker to youth groups nationwide and in Canada. She owns and operates a finishing school in Salt Lake City and directs a summer etiquette camp at Brigham Young University. She is a popular speaker for BYU's Especially for Youth program and Education Week, and she received the Outstanding Speaker of the Year award in 1989 from BYU Youth and Family Programs. A former Mrs. Utah America, she is well known for her sparkling personality and insight into today's social problems. *Dating, Dining, Dancing, and Other Teen Dilemmas* is her first published book.

Vivian is the wife of S. Douglas Cline, and they are the parents of five children. The family resides in Draper, Utah.

A longtime friend of the author, Carol Warnick was instrumental in the conceptualization and editing of this book. She graduated with honors from the University of

Wyoming College of Law and is a lawyer specializing in estate planning for a firm in Casper, Wyoming. She is a frequent speaker to community and professional groups.

Thomas R. Leishman is a recent graduate of Taylorsville High School in Taylorsville, Utah. He was the recipient of the 1994 Sterling Scholar Award for Art at Taylorsville High School and has received several other awards at the district level for his illustrations. As a senior, he won a nationwide contest to be art director for one week at Channel One, a national educational news channel based in Los Angeles.

I hope you have enjoyed reading this book as much as I have enjoyed writing it. If you have any questions on etiquette or social skills that I can help you with, or if you would like me to speak to your school, club, church, or civic organization, please feel free to write me:

Vivian Cline
P. O. Box 522
Draper, Utah 84020